Aquila:
The Adventures
of a Young Girl

LUCY HOBBS

To My Dear Alison
thank you So much
for being a good
customer & friend

All the best

Amy xxx

The Adventures of a Young Girl

Aquila

Design StoryTerrace

Copyright © Lucy Hobbs

First print November 2021

StoryTerrace

www.StoryTerrace.com

CHAPTER ONE

Aquila, at only 21 years of age, has big dreams of becoming an entrepreneur.

But how can I do that? she sighs, touching the silky fabric of her translucent negligee. *One day I will find my handsome, wealthy Prince Charming!* she thinks, heading into the bedroom for her usual bed-time routine.

Every night, in front of her mirror, Aquila brushes her long, dark, shiny hair. As she does so, her troubles melt away and her mind drifts towards the dreams she has nurtured since she was a teenager: dreams of Prince Charming; dreams of riches; dreams of success.

"One day, I will find my Prince Charming!" she says, out loud, to her reflection. "A very handsome and wealthy man who will spoil me rotten. He'll buy me expensive designer clothes, flowers, chocolates, handbags, purses… He'll shower me with gifts… And he'll love me with all his heart, no matter what!" Aquila smiles and walks over to her bed, laying down and staring at the ceiling, her mind full of opulent fantasies.

Aquila is a very ambitious, sweet and innocent young girl. People have been telling her this ever since she was a toddler – from her beloved grandmother to her favourite teacher, Diane. She is also a very pretty girl, with a heart of gold just like her mother's. She lives with her parents – Mr and Mrs Lawrence – and is their only child. Though they longed for more children, more children never came. During a consultation with the family doctor, they were told that Mr Lawrence's alcoholism might be the reason that Aquila's mother couldn't get pregnant again. Nevertheless, Aquila's father continued to drink.

Aquila's mother, Cristina, works with a wealthy family – the Jones' – as a part-time nanny. As rich as the Jones family may be, Cristina doesn't earn very much for her work. It's enough to support her family, but not enough to rid them of their financial worries. Aquila's father, Robert, is a self-employed taxi driver, but his earnings haven't been great lately, either, due to an outbreak of the flu.

"People nowadays are too scared to go out. It's just that time again, I guess. Seasonal flu outbreak!" Robert scoffs to his wife, settling down at the table with his usual wine bottle in hand.

"Well, Robert, if you hadn't brought extra bottles of wine tonight it might not be such a problem. But I guess the red wine must come before the bills, right?" Cristina retorts, her venomous voice taking her weary husband by surprise.

"No... No... Cristina, here you go again! You always criticise me for having the smallest treat. Why do you always need to criticise my little habit?"

"*'Little'* habit?" Cristina sneers. "If this is what you call a *little* habit, Robert, I'd hate to see a 'big' one!"

"No, no, no. Cristina, since we've been married you've always been against my drinking. It's just not for you – fine! But for me, it helps me with my stress!"

"Stress? Maybe you wouldn't have so much stress if you didn't spend all of our spare cash on wine!"

The bright, clever young Aquila – still lying on her bed and daydreaming about her future – listens absentmindedly to her parents bickering about their financial situation and her father's addiction to alcohol. For as long as she can remember, her parents have always had financial problems, and they have always argued about her father's drinking.

How I wish I could help my parents, she thinks. At their age, they should be relaxing and taking it easy. They're too old for these petty squabbles. Maybe, when I find my Prince Charming, he'll help me to take all of my parents' troubles away...

Aquila's thoughts are still full of these fantasies as she drifts off into a peaceful sleep.

*

The young girl is aiming to become a successful businesswoman when the time is right. This is a fact which she often shares with her Business teacher, Diane, and her best friend, Charlotte.

"Hey! Aquila! Look at that thing!" Charlotte shouts to her best friend, as they play badminton on the street outside their houses the following day.

"What, Charlotte? What am I supposed to be looking at?" Aquila replies, glancing round.

"My Aunt Betty and my Uncle Paul are visiting... Look at their fancy car. Aunty Betty calls it a *Lambo*. Why is the car called a Lambo!?"

"It's short for Lamborghini," Aquila replies, thinking that one day she would like to have at least two Lamborghinis of her own. One for her and one for her Prince Charming. Hers would be baby blue, and his… Well, his could be whatever colour he liked, so long as he was paying for them both.

"Aunty Betty married Uncle Paul in Las Vegas 35 years ago. He was a wealthy businessman in America but he gave it up and settled here in the UK to be with my aunt!" Charlotte explains, cheerfully, as they pass the shuttlecock lazily between them. "They have two kids too – my cousins – but I haven't seen them in ages. They're studying at Harvard.

"Uncle Paul has settled in really well though, since he moved to the UK," Charlotte continues. (She can always be counted on to make conversation.) "All the neighbours love him, because at the weekends, he goes to the local pub and buys everyone beer. And he helps young people living on the streets to get on their feet by giving them jobs at his car dealership. It's near Soho."

"Oh wow! That's very kind of him," Aquila replies to her friend, just as she strikes the shuttlecock, sending it arcing high into the sky.

"Anyway… Aquila, my friend, I have a favour to ask you…"

"Oh yeah? And what kind of favour might that be, 'my friend'? You wouldn't be about to try and persuade me to go along with some ridiculous plan of yours, would you?" Aquila replies, raising her eyebrows in response to Charlotte's cheeky smile.

Charlotte's face reddens. "You know me too well, Aquila."

"Of course I do," Aquila says with a grin. "You've been making that cheeky face since primary school!"

Charlotte smiles even more. "Ok, ok!" she says.

"But it better be good this time!" Aquila tells her. "If I remember correctly, last time you used that face, it was because you wanted to go and have 'a fun day out in the park', and I ended up getting dog poo all over my new designer trainers! The only new pair of trainers I've ever owned, ruined!"

Charlotte's grin becomes a mixture of contrition and amusement. "Ok, ok, it's not going to be like that, I promise!"
"Then why are you laughing? Charlotte?"

"Because… I'm remembering the dog poo incident!

It was horrendous!"

"It was!"

"Do you remember how you threw a big lump of mud at me? And we didn't speak for days because I thought you were throwing dog poo at me! And when we did speak again, we kept crying and crying because we'd missed each other so much?"

"It was a pretty powerful bonding experience!" Aquila concedes. "We never argued ever again."

"Until now, probably…"

"No, no, go on, what is it?"

"Would you like to come to Aunty Betty's party? Next weekend? It's her 60th birthday! There's going to be a lot of booze! Cake, chocolate, games… Plus, there are supposed to be some handsome guys who work with Uncle Paul coming along. Some of them are even coming over from America! You never know… we might find our soulmates, right?"

"Umm…" Aquila is hesitant.

"C'mon, Aquila! This is a once in a lifetime

opportunity for both of us! And I want to see my cousins too, and you can finally meet them as well. Remember Georgia? My cousin? She went to our primary school."

"Yes, I remember her..."

"So what do you say? It'll be so fun, Aquila!"

"Hmm. No, thanks," Aquila says, at last, though she isn't entirely sure why the prospect of a party with her best friend is troubling her.

"What? Why?"

"Because... I have to study – I have Business and Literature work to do." Aquila feels a strange sensation in her gut when she thinks about the party. Why? Why can't she just smile, relax and tell her friend that she can't wait to party with her? Isn't that what a normal 21-year-old would do?

"Nonsense! I have to do mine too, but it can wait until the bank holiday is over! Come on, Aquila, you're always saying that you're desperate to meet your Prince Charming. This could be your chance!"

Aquila sighs. If she wants to be a successful

entrepreneur, she needs to study. But if she wants to meet her Prince Charming, won't she have to go to a few parties, too? "Ok, you've convinced me," she tells her friend at last.

"Yes!" Charlotte cheers, delightedly, and starts dancing in the street goofily, twirling her badminton racquet in the air above her head. "See... I knew you'd want to go as much as I do, and I promise you my friend: it will be fun, fun, fun!"

"Okay...okay…" says Aquila, as she prepares to serve the shuttlecock. "You got me to say yes. Now leave me alone before I change my mind!"

"Okay, okay!" Charlotte replies, grinning. "Party girls, here we come!"

*

At 21 years of age, young Aquila has a natural, sleek beauty. As she steps into the kitchen to show her mother her party outfit – a short black dress which clings to her curves, the neckline swooping down past her cleavage, almost to her belly button – Cristina frowns.

"Don't you think that's a bit too much, darling?"

she asks her daughter, gently, as Aquila walks back and forth in front of the large mirror in the hallway.

"What do you mean, Mum?"

"Well, I mean your outfit. The amount of... flesh on show. Don't you think it's a bit... much? Mightn't it attract the wrong sort of attention?"

"Oh, Mother. Back in your day, maybe you felt like you had to wear jeans or baggy trousers to parties. But maybe that's why you only pulled a drunken waste of space like Dad. But in the 21st Century, this dress is the kind of dress you wear if you want to find the man of your dreams. Believe me."

Cristina's eyes widen at her daughter's outburst. "That's a bit harsh, young lady," she replies, clearly irritated. "Without your 'drunken' dad, you wouldn't be here in this world."

"Mother! Calm down, I'm just joking," Aquila says, kissing Cristina on both cheeks. "Sorry... I think I'm just a bit nervous about the party. Besides anything else, I'm going to be late if I don't leave right now!"

"But darling, you still haven't told me what party

you're going to, or where it is!"

"I have, Mum. I told you the other day. I'm going to Charlotte's Aunt Betty's 60th birthday party. It's in Soho!"

"What? Soho? You didn't tell me that."

"Yes I did…"

"No you –"

Beep…Beeeppp! The insistent sound of Charlotte's car horn cuts Cristina off before she can finish.

"Bye, Mum. Charlotte's here." Aquila is grabbing her bag and keys and running out of the door before her mother has the chance to argue the fact that her precious daughter is heading all the way to central London for a party, in a dress that's cut down to her belly button.

"Okay, okay. But you two be careful and watch each other's backs!"

"Of course we will. Bye, Mum." Aquila steps back into the hallway to kiss Cristina on the cheek.

"Bye darling. Enjoy, have fun and be good!"

"Thanks, Ma!" Aquila says, but the smirk on her face tells Cristina that her daughter has no intention of 'being good'.

Well, Cristina thinks to herself, as the sound of Charlotte's car disappears down the road, *I suppose I was no different when I was her age...*

CHAPTER TWO

"Hey, Aquila, are you ready?" Charlotte calls impatiently from her car as her best friend totters down her driveway, struggling to walk elegantly in six-inch stilettos. "C'mon, jump in! Are you excited?"

"Of course I am!" Aquila replies, clambering into the car and buckling up her seat belt. "This is my first big party ever since we were little. I can't wait!" It's true that Aquila feels excited, but she still can't shake off the feeling in her gut that something bad might be about to happen. *It's just butterflies,* she tells herself. *Pull yourself together, Aquila.*

"I can't wait either," Charlotte replies, concentrating as she reverses the car off of Aquila's driveway. "I can't wait to get drunk!"

Charlotte begins to laugh, and Aquila finds herself laughing along with her.

"This is going to be so much fun," Charlotte

continues. "Just me and my BFF, the Young Aquila..." Charlotte adopts a funny voice as she uses this old nickname.

"Hey! Don't call me 'the Young Aquila'!" Aquila protests. "You know I hate it! Besides, I'm not so young anymore!"

Charlotte rolls her eyes at Aquila's sensitivity. "In fairness," she says, "I am older than you by three days. So technically... I can call you the Y-O-U-"

Laughing, Aquila slaps her best friend's arm affectionately before she can continue. "Hey! I told you! Don't even THINK of calling me that name again."

"Ok, ok! You're the boss! If the boss wants to be yaaaawn inducingly boring, that's her prerogative!"

"Good!" Aquila replies, choosing not to rise to her friend's mockery. "Now will you behave yourself and keep your eyes on the road?"

Aquila has barely finished her sentence when Charlotte slams on the brakes and the car comes to a stop with an almighty BANG.

For a moment, the two of them say nothing, their heavy breathing the only sound to break the silence. Then, at last, Charlotte speaks.

"Woah! Sorry, but that totally wasn't my fault... I mean that driver was an IDIOT and got WAY too close to me and now he's just going to SPEED off like nothing happened? I mean, the CHEEK of that –"

"Charlotte?"

"Yeah?"

"Look, nobody's hurt, ok? Shall we just... go? And, maybe... you could try and concentrate on the road?" Aquila's heart is pounding hard in her chest, but part of her is relieved by Charlotte's near crash. *That must have been what my bad feeling was about,* she tells herself. *Maybe now I can relax and enjoy the party.*

*

The rest of the drive takes place in silence until, eventually, the girls pull up outside the house of Charlotte's Aunty Betty: a great, four-storey Georgian mansion that would be expensive anywhere in the world, let alone in the heart of Soho. Aquila can hardly believe that a house this grand exists in a place like this.

"Wow. This place is huge." Aquila says. "How have you never brought me here before?"

"I know, right? And look at all of those beautiful cars!"

Charlotte gestures towards the array of Lamborghinis, Porsches and Ferraris that line the pavements outside the house, glittering and sparkling in the early evening sunlight.

"Amazing," Aquila says, quietly. *How I wish*, she thinks to herself, *that I could have just one of those cars for myself.*

"Hurry! Hurry!" Charlotte is already bustling out of the driver's side of the car. "My cousin just texted me... My uncle is about to give his big speech!"

*

"Ladies and gentlemen, let's celebrate this beautiful wife of mine," Charlotte's Uncle Paul is saying, as they walk into the gorgeously landscaped gardens and join the crowd of guests. "Betty and I have been married for 35 years, and I still believe that she is the most gorgeous woman in the whole world."

The garden fills with the gentle sound of polite clapping.

"Thank you, thank you. Way back then, young and naive as I was, all I wanted was to find my soulmate. And how lucky was I, foolish kid as I was, to meet the woman of my dreams, this beautiful English rose wandering through the crazy streets of Las Vegas?"

"You're lucky I didn't meet her first!" one man calls out, drawing a burst of laughter from the crowd, and a chuckle of appreciation from the orator himself.

"Well, maybe I am," Paul says, generously, before turning to face his wife. "Betty, I followed you halfway across the world – from the bright lights of Nevada to the heart of the English capital. I don't regret it for a minute, and if you wanted me to follow you halfway around the world all over again, I'd do it in a heartbeat."

Betty smiles coyly, and a collective romantic sigh emanates from the women in the crowd. Uncle Paul raises his glass and smiles.

"To my beautiful wife! May she be blessed with many more happy birthdays!"

"To Betty!" the crowd cheers, raising their glasses in response.

Once the clapping and cheering has died down, Uncle Paul speaks one more time.

"Ok. I could talk all night about the wonder that is my wife, but hey, it's time to celebrate. Everybody, help yourself to a drink and let's dance!"

*

"Wow," Aquila says, between sips of a spectacularly strong mojito that Charlotte has somehow magically produced from thin air. "Your aunt and uncle are so in love."

"I know," Charlotte replies, chugging her mojito down in three long gulps. "It's so cute. Life goals, eh? OOF, BRAIN FREEZE! Hey, Aquila, do you mind if I go and find my cousins quickly? Just to say 'hi'? I won't be long, I promise!"

"Of course, no problem. I'll see you in a bit," Aquila replies, taking a slow sip of her drink as Charlotte disappears among the thronging mass of party guests.

After a moment, Aquila walks away from the crowd and into the house. She finds herself stepping into a beautiful Art Deco hallway, the walls lined with antique mahogany chairs and expensive looking oil paintings. Gently, she runs her fingertips along the rough texture of one of the paintings, feeling the bumps and grooves of the ancient paint. *Wow*, she thinks to herself. *How I wish I could have just one painting like this. Even a single one of these must cost more money than I've ever seen in my life...*

At that moment, lost in thought, Aquila is pulled out of her reverie by the sound of a polite cough.

"Ahem!"

Aquila spins around, startled, and her eyes land upon a man – a much older man, sharply dressed in a classic tuxedo – standing before her.

"Excuse me, miss, I'm so sorry to startle you. But could I possibly offer you a drink?" the man asks, in a voice as smooth and rich as espresso.

"Do I recognise you?" Aquila asks, frowning. There's something familiar about this man. "Oh, wait! Aren't you the guy who shouted out just now during Paul's speech?"

The man smirks wryly. "Well, I wouldn't exactly describe it as shouting," he says, his eyes sparkling with humour. "Whoever that man was, I'm sure he was just showing his appreciation for a beautiful woman."

"So it wasn't you?" Aquila replies, taken aback by this enigmatic response.

The man's smirk grows broader. "Come on, now," he says, his voice full of flirtation. "You don't really have me confused with that arrogant – albeit handsome – chap, do you?"

Aquila smiles bashfully but says nothing. *What is this guy's deal?* She thinks, but there isn't much time to ponder before he continues speaking.

"My name, by the way, is Donald," the man says. "Donald Smith."

"I'm Aquila. Aquila Lawrence."

"Aquila? What a beautiful name. I don't think I've ever met an Aquila before. But then, I suppose, a woman as singularly beautiful as you ought to have a name as remarkable as Aquila."

Aquila can feel the blush rushing to her cheek, and she hopes that her makeup is powerful enough to conceal it. "Thank you, Donald."

"You're welcome. Anyway, what is a beautiful woman such as yourself doing all alone at a party like this?" Donald asks, taking a step closer to Aquila.

"I'm not alone. I'm with a friend."

Donald glances around at the empty hall and smiles again.

"Well, I mean I'm waiting for my friend to come back. I thought I'd have a walk around and see if there was anything interesting inside."

"Well, you certainly made the right decision. Here I am."

"Some random old guy wasn't exactly what I had in mind," Aquila snaps back, and her hand rushes to her

25

face as she realises that her mouth has run away with her. "I'm sorry, I didn't mean –" *It's the mojito…* Aquila thinks to herself. *I've forgotten how to hold my tongue!*

"Hey," Donald says, seemingly unruffled by Aquila's insult. "I may be old but I still know how to have fun. So how about that drink, my lady?"

Donald offers a hand to Aquila. *My lady*, she thinks to herself. *He's talking to me like I'm royalty or something.* She decides to take his hand.

"Ok," she says, sweetly. "Just one drink."

As Aquila and Donald step into the garden, she can feel his eyes on her. He's playing the gentleman – cool and confident – but he can't hide the desire burning in his eyes. The feeling of it sends a thrill through her whole body, and as he touches her elbow to guide her towards the drinks table, it sends a shot of electricity racing through to her fingertips.

"With my young heart, I assure you, you won't be bored tonight, Aquila. I will be your servant for the entire night, and you can be my princess. If it pleases you, my lady."

Aquila's heart is pounding; she's never had this much attention in her life. She can't let Donald know this though, so she takes a deep breath and does her best to play it cool.

"Ok, I don't mind. If that's what you want."

"It's what I want."

Donald pours Aquila a glass of champagne and mixes himself an Old Fashioned cocktail. Then, passing her the champagne flute, he proposes a toast.

"To beautiful evenings and beautiful people," he says, the wry smirk returning to his face. Aquila has a strange feeling that there is something behind that smirk. Something mysterious or even cruel.

"To beautiful evenings and beautiful people," she echoes, clinking her glass against his and sipping her champagne.

"Why don't we take these drinks out to the front of the house, so that I can show you my car?"

*

All thoughts of Charlotte – and where she might have gone – have flown from Aquila's mind as she stands in front of Donald's beautiful Rolls Royce. The car seems to shimmer and sparkle in the late evening sunlight, and there isn't a speck of dirt to be seen on the silver coloured paint.

"Would you like to come inside?" Donald asks, touching his hand lightly to Aquila's lower back. "There's a surprise I'd love to show you."

"What is it?" Aquila asks, curious, but Donald says nothing. He only smirks.

Aquila throws caution to the wind and, tentatively, lets Donald lead her to the passenger door. He opens it and, demurely, she climbs inside. Quickly, Donald shuts the door, walks round to the other side of the car and gets into the driver's seat.

"Fancy going for a drive?" he asks.

"Is that the surprise?" Aquila asks.

"No. The surprise is that there's a rather expensive wine collection in the back. If you come for a drive with me, perhaps I'll show it to you."

"You're a wine collector?" Aquila asks, curious.

"I collect a lot of beautiful things," Donald says, and his words hang in the air like electricity.

CHAPTER THREE

"So, tell me more about yourself." Donald says, as Betty and Paul's mansion recedes into the distance behind them.

Aquila can't quite believe she's said yes to this unanticipated excursion. She's never left a party with a stranger before. She's never been alone with a man like Donald before. She's never drunk a 50-year old glass of vintage wine while sitting in a car before, either. Today is clearly a day for trying new things. *The cocktails have gone to my head*, she thinks. *I hope Charlotte doesn't start to worry about me...*

"What kind of things do you want to know?" she asks Donald, sipping her wine. It tastes the same as the cheap wine she and Charlotte drink, but she doesn't say this to Donald. Perhaps it's her unrefined palate that can't tell the difference.

"I want to know what it is that you want in life so that I can know what to give you."

Aquila feels her cheeks blushing again. *Are older men always this confident and assertive?*

"I want a lot of things," Aquila says eventually.

"Well, that's good to hear, because unlike most men… I have a lot to give," Donald replies.

Aquila isn't quite sure what to say to this, so she says nothing. Instead, she watches out of the car window as they turn through quiet streets lined with tall, white Georgian villas. *I'd always thought of Soho as incredibly busy.* She thinks to herself, remembering the occasional theatre trips she took as a child with her parents. The streets had been full of tourists, partygoers and street performers. Here, everything is tranquil and silent. *This much peace in such a prime location must come with a hefty price tag*, Aquila thinks.

Eventually, after a few minutes without conversation, Donald breaks the silence.

"Listen, Aquila, I'm going to level with you. I make no secret of the fact that my life is filled with every single thing that I could want. Except for a beautiful woman to share it with. If I had a woman like you, I could happily spend the rest of my life showering her with whatever it took to make her happy. How's that wine?"

"It's delicious," Aquila lies.

"It's from the 1970s," Donald says. "A long time before you were even born, no?"

"My mother was born in the 1970s," Aquila replies, cheekily.

"Well, your mother and this wine are both fine vintages, I'm sure," Donald retorts, as they pull into the long, gravel driveway of his house. "But as much as I appreciate fine vintages, I have a great appreciation for younger things, too." With this last comment, Donald places his left hand lightly on Aquila's thigh. The metal of his wedding ring is cold against her bare skin.

"Are you married?" she asks, gesturing at the ring.

"I was," Donald says, with that same smirk creeping across his lips. "But it didn't work out."

Aquila wants to take in the grandeur of Donald's house – a great, Georgian mansion which makes Betty and Paul's house look like a pokey flat in comparison. The gravel driveway is lined by gorgeous topiary, and Grecian pillars stand either side of the vast double doors at the entrance of the house. It is impossibly grand, but she can hardly focus on it. All she can focus on is Donald's hand, grazing gently against her thigh, moving slowly towards the hem of her short dress.

"Aquila, tell me. What is it that I can give you? I'll give you anything you want..."

Donald's hand is moving further and further up her thigh, only an inch or two now from the lace hem of her underwear.

"Really? You'll give me anything I ask for?"

Donald nods vigorously, seemingly distracted by the sensation of Aquila's warm skin. "Anything," he murmurs.

The feeling of Donald touching her is making Aquila uneasy, so she grabs his hand and squeezes it. "Could you give me a tour of your house?" she says, with a voice that is more cheerful and less nervous than she feels. "Maybe you could show me some of your other collections?"

Donald smiles, and the magic spell of Aquila's thigh seems to have been broken, for the moment at least.

"Of course," he says, smiling warmly. "Where are my manners? Come on inside and I'll show you my art gallery. If you liked Paul's collection, you're going to love mine."

*

As Aquila wanders along the art-lined corridors of Donald's house, still nursing her glass of wine from the car, she thinks back to the classic car collection she glimpsed on the driveway outside. *He may not look like my Prince Charming*, she thinks, *but he's as rich as a prince. And he is charming, in his own way.*

The feeling of Donald's arm draping around Aquila's shoulder draws her out of her thoughts and back into the world of fine art.

"A penny for your thoughts, my lady?" he asks. "Are you thinking about my paintings? Or are you wondering how much you could sell them all for?"

There is something frightening about Donald, charming though he is. It's as though he needs to control every detail of their interaction: where they go; what they talk about; even the thoughts in Aquila's head. *You're being silly*, Aquila tells herself. *You're just scared because you've never been alone with a man before. Donald has been nothing but polite. Plus, he's RICH! Give him a chance, Aquila.*

"I was just thinking about this painting," she says, gesturing to a portrait of a beautiful young woman, her blonde hair tumbling over her delicate shoulders, her eyes staring out of the painting and right into Aquila's soul. "She's beautiful. So beautiful that it feels as though she's real."

"Even if she were real enough to step out of that painting and into this room, she still wouldn't be as beautiful as you, Aquila," Donald says.

"Stop," Aquila says. "You're making me blush." Truthfully though, she can't deny that Donald's attention is flattering.

"Is my attention too much for you, sweetheart?" he says, turning her body by the shoulders so that they are facing one another, then taking both of her hands in his. The skin of his hands is rough and unusually cold. "The truth is, I'm not a young man and, as such,

I don't like to waste my time. I know what I want, and I'm looking at it right now. It's not every day that a man – even a man as successful as me – comes across a beauty as exquisite as yours, Aquila. If you will agree to be mine, I will treat you like a princess every day from now on. I'll shower you with presents, I'll give you all the money you could want. I'll support your parents, too. All I need from you is for you to say that you'll be all mine, and that you might do your best to fall in love with me, the way that I'm falling in love with you."

My God, Aquila thinks, as Donald lifts her hand to his lips and kisses it tenderly. *He is not wasting any time!*

"Wow, Donald, I don't know what to say."

"Say you'll be my girlfriend," he says, without hesitation. "If you do, I'll buy you a brand new car tomorrow." He reaches into his pocket and pulls out a roll of crisp notes, then presses them into Aquila's hand. "Here's £1,000. You can go shopping and get yourself pampered while I get your car for you."

Can this be real? Aquila thinks. He may not look like Prince Charming, but he's offering me everything I've ever dreamed of.

"Ok, Donald, I'll be your girlfriend," she says.

Donald's face lights up with a smile so bright that, for a moment, he looks as sweet and innocent as a schoolboy.

"Oh, Aquila, you don't know how happy you've made me," he says.

For a moment, they stare at one another, neither one saying a thing. Just as Aquila thinks that she can't take the pressure anymore, Donald takes her chin in his hand and brings his face close to hers, so close that she can smell the red wine on his breath and the expensive aftershave on his neck. But then, just as their lips are about to meet, he pulls away.

"No, it's too soon," he says. "Too rushed. We should take our time."

He offers an arm to Aquila, and she takes it.

"Come, my princess. Let me take you on a tour of the rest of your new castle."

*

As Donald guides Aquila from room to room, showing her a library lined with floor-to-ceiling bookshelves and a state-of-the-art cinema room, an enormous wine cellar and a kitchen as big as Aquila's whole house, she thinks about the strange situation she has found herself in. *What will Charlotte think?* she wonders. *What will my parents think? Donald must be older than Dad! But surely, that won't matter to them when they realise how much Donald can help them. No more financial troubles, no more arguments about drinking and unpaid bills... It's as though I've been given everything I ever dreamed of, all in one night. All in this... partial Prince Charming.*

"Are you away with your thoughts again, my lady?" Donald asks.

It's as though every time Aquila thinks a dark thought about him, Donald can hear it.

"I was just thinking that I need someone to pinch my skin. I feel as though I'm walking through a dream. I can't wait to tell Charlotte tomorrow."

"Let's not think about tomorrow, just yet," Donald says. "I want to think about tonight."

CHAPTER FOUR

The tour of Donald's house seems to go on forever, but eventually they find themselves standing in his garden. Aquila can't see much in the dark, but it seems to sweep endlessly into the distance. They stand together in silence, arm in arm, until a flash of orange eyes makes Aquila jump.

"What was that?" she asks, her heart pounding.

Donald simply laughs. "That? It was a cat!" he says, pointing.

Aquila follows the line of his finger and spots the cat – black as midnight – crossing her path and sauntering away into one of the bushes in the distance.

"Is it yours?" she asks, embarrassed to realise that her heart is still pounding with fear.

"It's not mine. I don't know who it belongs to – I've never seen it before. I'm sorry you were frightened, sweetheart. Shall we go back inside? I realised I have one more room to show you."

Obediently, still a little shaken by the strange fear she had felt in the face of the black cat, Aquila follows Donald into the house.

"Which room?" she asks.

Donald says nothing. He simply guides her through the kitchen and into the hallway, then up the spiral staircase to a grand, oak door. Gently, he turns the handle and pushes the door aside to reveal a shadowy room furnished all in black: black curtains; black carpet; black walls. Looming large against the back wall, draped with sheets and pillows of black silk, is an enormous king-size bed.

Aquila feels a sinking sense of dread as she gazes into this lair, as black and mysterious as the bottom of the ocean, but she doesn't have long to explore the feeling. Instead, she is distracted by the jolting sensation of Donald's hand grabbing onto hers and tugging her firmly into the murky depths of the bedroom. Softly, the door clicks shut behind her. Aquila feels a rising panic in her throat as she is consumed by darkness. As the seconds pass, her eyes don't seem to adjust to the dark at all. It is as though all the light in the world has been utterly extinguished.

"This is now your bed, my lady. A bed fit for a princess, no?"

"It's… quite something," Aquila says, feeling almost lost for words. "I've only slept in a single bed before."

"Well that just won't do, will it?" Donald says, moving so that he is standing barely an inch behind Aquila. Lightly, his fingertips move to her hips and move slowly up towards her waist.

"This bed is all yours," he whispers, so close to her ear that she can feel the heat of his breath. "And you are all mine."

Donald kisses her neck now and, although she had been anticipating his touch, Aquila feels suddenly and keenly aware that she wants it to stop.

"Can we let some air in here?" she says, stepping forwards and pulling away from Donald's grip. "I'm so warm."

"Of course, my darling. Let's take our time and savour this moment," Donald replies, taking her hand

and guiding her forwards.

The dark is still completely consuming, and it isn't until she is within a few feet of them that the shadowy outline of the curtains becomes clear to Aquila. Donald steps to the side and pulls on a little rope which thrusts the curtains wide open, revealing an enormous window which runs from the floor to the ceiling. After a moment of fiddling in the dark, Donald forces the windows open, releasing a burst of fresh air. Aquila grasps onto the window frame and tilts her face towards the cool air of the night, breathing in deeply.

"I feel a little dizzy," she tells Donald, noticing that his hands are crawling back to her waist. This time, she notices, he grabs on a little more firmly. Aquila wonders if she'd be able to pull free this time.

"Dizzy, my darling?" Donald's voice has a note of concern but also impatience.

"Just a little," Aquila replies, though she's understating things somewhat. Really, she feels that if she doesn't keep holding onto the windowsill and focusing on her breathing, she might pass out.

"Perhaps it's the wine," Donald suggests.

Perhaps he's right, Aquila thinks. After all, I don't usually drink this much. But I don't usually feel this strange dread when I drink. I don't usually feel like my legs might give way beneath me.

"Perhaps," she replies. Speaking is starting to feel like an effort.

"Maybe a lie down on the bed would help?" Donald says, his hands gripping a little tighter to her waist.

Aquila focuses on the bright light of the crescent moon in the sky overhead, casting its glittering, romantic light on the garden below. She tries to calm herself by noting the things she can see. Stone statues and flowerbeds lining a quadrangle of neatly mown grass, a fountain at its centre. Tall trees to either side of her, cloaking the house in privacy. The gravel driveway, winding into the dark distance.

"I think I just need a little more air."

"Of course," Donald says, his voice leaning more towards impatience than sympathy now. Suddenly, his hands move from Aquila's waist to the small of her back, and she feels his hands working the delicate clasp of her dress. "Perhaps you need to cool down," he says, and he unhooks the clasp and begins, slowly, to draw down the zipper of her dress.

"Maybe I could have a glass of water?" Her voice comes out more meekly than she had intended. A mouse's squeak.

"Water, of course," Donald says, but he is clearly past the point of listening. "Aquila, your skin might be the most exquisite skin I have seen in my life."

Donald is kissing Aquila's neck now, more urgently and hungrily this time. She feels his teeth nibble lightly at the skin of her neck as his hands slip inside the back of her dress and reach forwards, grasping firmly at her breasts.

"Oh, Aquila," he murmurs between kisses, emitting moans and groans of pleasure, one hand squeezing her nipples so firmly that it sends a shooting pain through Aquila's body, the other venturing downwards over her ribcage, over the smooth skin of her stomach, past her belly button...

All of this seems to happen to Aquila in slow motion. Her mind feels sharp and alert, and she is aware of every sensation: the rough skin of his palm against her breasts; the heavy smell of alcohol on his breath; the low, tigerish growls of pleasure as he, predator-like, explores every inch of her body. But in spite of this hyper-awareness, Aquila is frozen in place. It is as though a spell has been cast and, try as she might, she is powerless to move so much as an inch.

"Aquila," he says, as his fingertips push past the hem of her lace underwear, "you are all mine now. Your smell... your body... your flesh... Every inch of you is so fresh and delicious... My body is so full of desire for you that I could eat you. And nobody would ever know..."

With this, Donald quickly pulls his hands out of Aquila's dress and, in one forceful motion, he rips it from her body and throws it to the ground at her feet.

"Donald, I –"

Aquila hears her tiny voice protesting Donald's advances with all the power and might of a butterfly.

"Shhh, Aquila, let's let our bodies do the talking." He grabs her waist again and squeezes so hard that it feels like a warning.

"Donald, I don't –"

"You are so beautiful, Aquila..." he interrupts, kissing her neck again, viciously, vampirically.

"Donald, please, can we just –"

This time, it's his hand that interrupts her, clasping so tightly over her mouth and nose that she can't breathe.

I have to do something, she thinks. *He's not going to stop unless I do something drastic.*

As Donald's other hand begins to wander downward again, Aquila's mind finally convinces her body to take action.

"Aghhhh!"

Suddenly, Donald lets go of Aquila and stumbles backwards, groaning with pain from the firm kick to the groin that Aquila, dizzy with relief, has delivered to him. She doesn't turn around. Instead, she keeps her eyes on the moon, steadying her breathing, listening to the sound of Donald moaning with pain. Then, she hears an almighty cracking sound, followed by a louder, more urgent cry of pain from Donald, followed by the thudding sound of his collapsing to the floor.

"Aquila, what have you done?" he says, his voice a strained croak.

The sound of Donald's voice seems to snap Aquila into action. She crouches down and gathers her torn dress, slipping quickly into it and hurriedly refastening the clasp. She turns to see his shadowy outline, crouched on the floor, one hand at his crotch, the other at his head.

"I was trying to tell you to stop!" she says, her voice firmer now.

"So try harder, you stupid bitch!" Donald spits, poisonously. "Look what you've done to my face!"

It's too dark for Aquila to look at anything, but she thinks she can see a slick shimmer of blood oozing from Donald's temple, glinting malevolently in the moonlight.

"I'm sorry!" she says, beginning to panic. "You had your hand on my mouth, I didn't know how to –"

This time it's Aquila who interrupts herself, as she watches Donald clumsily raise himself from the ground.

"You'll pay for this, you ungrateful little bitch," he spits, before turning away and moving towards the bed. Aquila watches with horror as he fumbles for something in the dark.

What is he looking for? Aquila thinks, moving stealthily towards the door. Or, at least, towards where she thinks the door is. Her body floods with relief as her fingers find the door handle, but the relief is quickly replaced by horror as she hears the unmistakable sound of metal scraping against metal. A knife. Realising there is no time to waste, Aquila turns the handle and the door swings open. The room floods with light and Aquila's heart floods with a dizzying sense of freedom – just as Donald's hand winds itself around her hair and pulls her back into the dark.

Pain sears through Aquila's body as she thrashes against Donald's grip.

"Hold still, you dumb little bitch!" Donald growls.

Aquila lunges so sharply at this that the two of them

crash to the ground together. She lands headfirst on the ground, Donald landing heavily on top of her, and a sharp pain blooms out so suddenly from her temple that she reaches out a finger to touch it. What she feels there is warm and wet. The last thing she sees as she fades into unconsciousness is a patch of blood pooling beneath her, sticky and dark. As she fades into the darkness, her head is full of Charlotte, of the cheerful party raging on a few miles away, and of whether or not the blood before her is her own or Donald's.

CHAPTER FIVE

"I'm not going to sleep," Robert says to his wife. "It's midnight. Where is Aquila? She said she'd be back by 11, didn't she?"

Cristina pours some more red wine into her husband's glass. It's not something she's normally willing to help her husband with, but this isn't a normal night. Cristina thinks that maybe, on this occasion, a little wine might help.

"Calm down, Robert," she says, gently. "Aquila is with Charlotte. She'll be fine. Yes, she said 11, but you know what teenagers can be like. She'll be back soon, I'm sure."

Cristina is intent on reassuring her husband, though, deep down, she knows it's herself that she's really hoping to reassure.

"Have you called her?"

"Yes, Robert. I've called her."

"And did she answer?"

"No, Robert. She didn't answer."

"Then why are you so sure that she's fine, *Tina?*"

All of a sudden, Robert lifts his wine glass into the air and hurls it at the wall. The violent sound of shattering glass smashing against the wall causes a shot of adrenaline to course through Tina's body.

"For God's sake, Robert. You're 55 years old. When are you going to grow up?" Cristina moves to collect the shards of glass, staring forlornly at the red wine stain seeping into her cream carpet. "Twenty years of marriage and you're still the same person you were back then. Was I an idiot to think you could ever change?"

"Oh, shut up," her husband replies.

What did I do to deserve this life? Cristina thinks, gathering the shards into a neat pile and wrapping them carefully in yesterday's newspaper. *We can't afford to pay our bills, let alone get new carpets. And I shouldn't be worrying about bills in my 50s – I should be retired, relaxing on a sunbed in Hawaii!*

She returns to the kitchen table to wait for her daughter, as her husband heads to the cupboard and pours himself a fresh glass of red wine.

*

"Aquila! Aquila?" Charlotte calls down yet another corridor of her aunty Betty's cavernous house. Yet again, the only reply she receives is silence.

Where the hell is she? Charlotte wonders.

"Excuse me, Aunty Betty?" Charlotte says, spotting her beloved aunt on her way into the kitchen. "Have you seen Aquila?"

"Oh hello there, my gorgeous little niece. How are you? Are you enjoying the party?"

Betty doesn't wait for an answer. Instead, she turns to the fridge and takes out a bottle of prosecco.

"I'm having a wonderful time, I was just wondering if –"

"I hate to be a bad influence," Betty interjects, "but would you like a little glass of this?"

"Um, ok, yes please, I just –"

"I saw you talking to your lovely cousins earlier – how fabulous for you to have such a catch up, eh?"

Betty turns to place a glass of prosecco in Charlotte's hand. It is so full that a glug of the sparkling wine spills as she places it in her niece's hand.

"It's been so lovely, but I was just wondering –"

"Cheers!"

"Cheers! I was just wondering if you'd seen Aquila, Aunty Betty?"

Finally, her aunt hears her question. "Aquila? Your lovely friend Aquila! You arrived with her just as Paul was giving his big speech!"

"Yes! That's her!"

"Well I saw her then, of course, but I can't say I've seen her for a while."

Charlotte's heart sinks. "Ok, well, thank you, Aunty."

"That's ok, my lovely. I'd better head outside and make sure that the stragglers are still enjoying their party. One a.m. and there's still a good crowd in the garden. Not bad for an old fogey like me, eh?"

"You're hardly an old fogey, Aunty," Charlotte says, flatly.

"Cheer up, chuck," Betty says, taking her niece's chin in her hand, affectionately. "Your friend will be fine. She probably just had too much to drink and headed home! People do that at parties all the time. You'll hear from her in the morning, I'm sure."

"You're probably right," Charlotte says, though there's a strong feeling in the depths of her stomach that says she's wrong.

"Wait! Was it you or was it Aquila that I saw talking to Paul's old colleague Donald?"

"Donald?"

"Yes, the old fellow. He's a bit odd but harmless, really. Absolutely minted and a bit weird about classic cars."

"I never met him," Charlotte says. "I think I'd remember a man like that."

"Well then, now that I think about it, that's who Aquila was with. I'm sure I saw the two of them talking together in the art gallery. That was a long time ago now, though."

"Ok," Charlotte says, her mind racing over the possibilities that this new piece of information opened up.

"Donald's an old gentleman and, like I say, he loves his cars. Maybe he dropped Aquila home to her parents," Betty offers, taking a long sip from her prosecco and turning to head towards the garden.

"Aunty Betty?" says Charlotte.

"Yes, darling?"

"I'm going to head off too, then," Charlotte says. "If Aquila turns up, will you let me know?"

"Of course, sweetheart. Oh, and take some food with you. We have loads left." Betty returns to Charlotte long enough to give her a quick kiss and a squeeze on the shoulder. "Thank you for coming tonight."

"No, thank you."

As Charlotte returns to her car, Tupperware containers full of leftovers in hand, she aches with guilt for leaving Aquila alone so early on in the party. *I'll visit her first thing in the morning,* she tells herself, as she clambers into the driver's seat. The smell of Aquila's perfume lingers in the car for the entire journey home.

CHAPTER SIX

Keep your eyes closed, Aquila tells herself, *and keep your breathing steady*. Pretending to be unconscious is the only strategy she can think of right now. The only thing that can buy her time to plan her escape.

"Didn't I tell you?" Donald says, as he gathers her into his arms and slings her over his shoulder in a fireman's lift. "You're mine now. You belong to me, and I will take you, whether you fight me or not."

Aquila focuses her energy on keeping her body limp and lifeless. *He's stronger than I'd imagined*, she thinks. *Was the dapper older gentleman act all for show?*

Suddenly, Donald lets go of Aquila and hurls her onto the king-size bed. The silk sheets – which had looked so appealing and luxurious only a short while ago – felt sticky and cloying against her skin, as though she were a fly trapped in a spider's web.

Donald was tugging Aquila's dress off, yanking her

up into an upright position and pulling the dress over her head. Aquila let her body flop back onto the bed, helpless, as Donald turned his attention to removing her bra.

"How can something so beautiful be so cruel?" he muttered to himself. "I offered you everything and you accepted, and this is the thanks I get?"

Aquila's eyes are still closed when she feels the weight of Donald leave the bed. Tentatively, she opens an eye to see where he's gone, but it's still completely dark in the bedroom. The curtains are closed again, so even the light of the moon is gone.

She doesn't know how long she's got before he returns, so she does the only thing she can do. Stealthily, she slips off the bed and onto the floor, where she crouches and removes her stiletto.

She stays there for a few moments, silent and alert as a prey animal, her whole body tuned to the sound of Donald rustling for something in the corner. The rustling stops, a lid slams shut, Donald's footsteps move towards the bed again.

"Now, young lady, these should make sure that

you don't start being a naughty girl and resisting me again," he says, clambering back onto the bed.

It's now or never, Aquila thinks. *This is my chance.*

BANG!

Aquila brings her stiletto down hard, using Donald's voice to guide her movement. Judging by the shrieking sound of pain and the hardness of the crashing contact, she has gotten lucky and hit his head.

For good measure, and without thinking too deeply about it, she raises her arm again and brings the stiletto down a second time.

CRACK!

This time, Donald doesn't make a sound. The room is silent, but for the ragged, petrified breaths that are emerging, unbidden, from Aquila's mouth.

"Donald?" she says, almost whispering, but there is no reply.

He's unconscious, she thinks. Dead, maybe, but she pushes this thought to the back of her mind. She can't start worrying that she's a murderer. She has to get out.

Scrabbling around frantically on the bed, she scoops up her bedraggled dress and slips it on again, though the clasp and zip are both now broken. She fumbles with the buckle of her stiletto for a moment, then feels her way through the dark until she reaches the door.

As it swings open, the room floods with light and her heart floods with relief. Only briefly, she glances back at the lifeless shape of Donald on the bed before leaving the bedroom and shutting the door firmly behind her.

*

It takes a while – weaving through unfamiliar corridors and being confronted with locked doors – but Aquila eventually makes her way out onto the front porch. She stands between the stone pillars which, only an hour or so ago, she had admired so earnestly. *How naive*, Aquila thinks to herself, but there is no time for self-flagellation. The gravel driveway out of Donald's house is long, winding into darkness, and she has no idea where it leads to.

It is only now that she realises that she has left her handbag in the house, with her phone inside.

I can't go back in there, she thinks to herself. *I'll have to rely on myself.*

It's a struggle walking along the gravel drive in stilettos, but the adrenaline coursing through Aquila's body seems to power her on relentlessly, lending her the stamina of an Olympic athlete. She starts to run, only stopping once when she sees a flash of orange light in her peripheral vision and dares to dream that it might be the headlight of a car.

"Hello?" she calls, torn between speaking loudly enough to be heard and quietly enough to avoid Donald, should he wake up.

Meow comes the reply. The glint of orange light comes closer, and she realises that it's the same black cat she'd seen earlier in the garden.

"Oh hello, little one," Aquila says, crouching down and stroking the cat's soft black fur. "You tried to warn me, didn't you?"

The cat nuzzles gently against Aquila's hand, and

she wonders if she should try and take the poor cat with her. But before she can scoop it into her arms, the cat stalks off into the dark. Aquila continues along the driveway.

At last, the driveway emerges onto a country lane. *Who knew there were lanes like this so close to Soho?* Aquila thinks to herself, wondering whether she should turn left or right. *How long was I in that car with him?*

She stares outwards into the shadowy dark. Left or right? Left or right? A faint glimmer of light in the far distance tells her to head left.

Soon enough, the country lane becomes a busier road. There are no streetlights, but at least this road is painted with markings. Gingerly, she turns left and begins walking along the road.

Three minutes later, the unmistakable glare of headlights emerges in the distance.

"HELP!" she yells, stepping into the road and waving. "HELP ME, PLEASE!"

Her heart is pounding as the car approaches, its appearance masked by the blinding light, but it doesn't slow. For a moment, she wonders if the driver could be Donald and if he could be about to take his revenge by hitting her. But no. The car merely swerves into the other lane and continues into the night.

Aquila keeps walking. This time, the road stays silent for what seems like an eternity. Minute after minute passes in total silence, Aquila's vision adjusting more and more to the gentle moonlight. Occasionally, the silence is disturbed by the flap of a bird's wing or the rustling of a creature in the grass verge, but mostly, Aquila is completely alone.

Eventually, another set of headlights crests the horizon. *Here goes nothing*, Aquila thinks, and she steps out into the middle of the road once more.

"Help! Help me please!" she yells, waving her arms frantically.

To her surprise, the car slows and comes to a stop. Nervously, she approaches, and the driver's window rolls slowly down.

"Good evening," she says, tremulously, to the man at the wheel.

"Good evening," the voice replies. It's too dark to make out much of the man's face, but the note of concern in his voice puts her at ease. "What on earth is a young lady like you doing out alone on a road like this at this time?"

"I... I..." Aquila wants to explain but the words catch in her throat.

"This is no safe place for anybody at two o'clock in the morning, let alone a young lady all on her own."

"Please don't call me young lady," Aquila says, her voice practically a whimper. She hadn't intended to snap at the driver, but the word 'lady' – used so liberally by Donald less than an hour ago – had induced a visceral reaction in her.

"I'm sorry. What's your name?"

"Aquila."

"What a beautiful name."

"It's Latin for eagle," Aquila says, her voice sounding as pitiful as a little girl.

AQUILA: THE ADVENTURES OF A YOUNG GIRL

"And how can I help you, Aquila? Are you going to tell me what has happened to you?"

Still, Aquila cannot make out the shadowy face of the stranger. Still, she cannot find the words to explain what has happened to her.

"I need to get back to the town centre so that I can catch a taxi to my friend's house. Can you help me?" she says, meekly, at last.

"Well, of course," the man replies. "I'd be glad to help. I wouldn't feel good about leaving you standing here on the road in the middle of the night. But really, didn't anybody ever tell you that it isn't a good idea to go getting in cars with strange men?"

"Please," Aquila says, desperately. "I don't know what else to do."

The driver pauses for a moment before leaning over to the passenger side and opening the door.

"Get in, little eagle," he says.

For a while, the pair drive in silence. Aquila feels a sense of peace and relief flooding her body as the dark road leads to a street-lit one, and hints of civilisation – road signs, roundabouts, bus stops – begin to re-emerge.

"I'm Dave, by the way," the driver says at last.

"Hi, Dave," Aquila replies, turning to offer the man a bashful smile.

To her surprise, Aquila's weak smile is met with a horrified grimace.

"My God," Dave says. "Your face! You're bleeding! What on earth happened to you out there?"

Aquila's hand moves to her temple, where blood is congealing and matting into her hair.

"I... I will explain," Aquila says. "Can you give me a moment?"

"Of course," Dave replies, though the concern on his face remains. "If you look in the glove compartment, there's a bottle of water, if you're thirsty. And some wipes, if you'd like to clean your face a little."

Gratefully, Aquila opens the glove compartment

and finds the items in question.

"Thanks," she says, finishing the entire bottle of water in two long gulps. "I didn't realise how thirsty I was. Hey, that's pretty organised, having this stuff in your glove compartment."

"Well, I can't take credit for that," Dave says, his voice wistful. "My wife is the organised one. Well, she was."

"Was?" Aquila says. "Sorry, I don't mean to pry."

"That's alright," Dave replies. "She passed away. Almost three years ago, now. Cancer. It was quite sudden, but quite painless – for her, at least."

"I'm so sorry," Aquila says. She studies his face and realises that Dave is really quite handsome. Too young to have suffered so much grief.

"Thank you," Dave says. "I suppose I ought to have moved on by now, but it's hard. Sometimes, I still can't believe it, you know? That she's gone. That's why I'm out driving in the middle of the night: sometimes I find myself staring at the ceiling, struggling to sleep, and I just have to get out of the house."

The two of them are silent for a while. Aquila realises that, as they approach the familiar sights of Soho, she doesn't want their time together to be over just yet. She's intrigued to know more about this strange, sad man, driving aimlessly in the night as he grieves his lost love.

"Have you got any children, Dave?" she asks.

"No, I haven't."

"Why not?" she asks, and immediately regrets the bluntness of her question. "I mean... Had you not been married very long?"

"Seven years last Thursday," Dave replies. "I guess that's why I've been struggling so much with sleep this week in particular."

"Oh. I'm... I'm just so sorry."

"It's ok," he says, with a brave smile. "My wife couldn't conceive. It was a difficult reality for us both to face, but perhaps it was never meant to be. No baby should grow up without a mother."

"I guess you're right," Aquila says. "I can't really

imagine the responsibility of motherhood."

"Aquila, if you don't mind me asking, how old are you?"

"I'm 21. Since last week."

"Wow. You've got your whole life ahead of you, eh? You're making me feel old Aquila. I just turned 35."

"Well, you don't look 35! You look 22 to me."

"Flattery will get you everywhere, Aquila."

Aquila feels her cheeks flush red, and is grateful for the darkness of the car. *Is he flirting with me?* she thinks, feeling a rush of pleasure at the idea. It's hard to believe that – only an hour or so ago – she was fighting for her life with Donald. Now, she's sitting in a comfortable car, safely returning to London, chatting to a handsome and kind man. He may not be as wealthy as Donald but he clearly has a good heart.

"You seem like a very sweet girl, Aquila. I don't like the idea of someone as good as you walking the streets in the middle of the night, all alone and covered in blood."

Aquila takes a deep breath and decides to pour her heart out to Dave. She tells him everything: meeting Donald at the party, agreeing to go back to his house with him, the dizziness, the violence, running for her life. It feels good to get it off of her chest, and once she's started, she can't seem to stop talking. By the time she finishes, Dave has pulled over into a parking space in a quiet side road, not far from Leicester Square.

"I was an idiot to go back with him, I know," she says. "It was stupid and naive."

"No amount of naivety is an excuse for the way he treated you, Aquila. What that man did to you was –"

"GET OUT OF THE CAR!"

It's a male voice that interrupts Dave's words, and not one she's heard before. Aquila turns towards it just in time to see a silhouette of a man standing in front of Dave's parked car, a gun pointed squarely in her direction, his finger squeezing the trigger.

CHAPTER SEVEN

Somehow, the odds are in Aquila and Dave's favour, and the bullet misses the windscreen. The deafening bang of the gunfire is followed by a deathly silence, before the man with the gun begins to approach the car, two other men emerging from the shadows behind him.

"Get out of the car, now!" the gunman growls, his pistol pointed directly at Dave.

Aquila notices that the two men behind him are armed, too. One has a baseball bat, the other a glinting blade. As they step forwards, it becomes clear that all three are wearing balaclavas.

"Get out of the car!" the man repeats. "Or I'll shoot you in the face."

"Oh my God," Aquila whispers, terrified. "Dave, who are these men?"

"I don't know, Aquila," Dave whispers back, his

voice surprisingly calm. "But let's stay cool. These windows are tinted, so they don't know who's inside. Before I wind down the window, I want you to crawl into the floorspace in the back. Be as quick and quiet as you can, and whatever you do, don't say ANYTHING once I wind down the window."

Deep in her gut, Aquila knows she can trust Dave. Obediently, she follows his instructions to the letter, until she is pressed flat against the floor of the backseat, the only sound the furious beating of her heart.

She hears Dave roll the window down.

"What's happening here, gentlemen?" Dave says, as calmly as a man ordering a McDonalds drive-through meal. "Is there a problem I should know about?

"Have you seen a young woman?"

"A young woman?" Dave replies, innocently. "What kind of young woman?"

He's a pretty convincing actor, Aquila thinks. *He'd have fooled me. But then… Donald fooled me, too.*

"Yes, a young woman. She was last seen on a road

that you've just driven from. There weren't many cars beside yours on that road, so we followed you here."

"You followed me here? Well, I'm very sorry, gentlemen," Dave replied, smoothly. "But I think you've probably wasted your time."

He's so smooth and calm, Aquila thinks, but her train of thought is quickly interrupted by the men pulling Dave's car door open and violently dragging him out onto the street. Aquila's heart races wildly, and she prays silently that the men won't spot her in the backseat.

Somehow, even as he's being manhandled and threatened by three strange men with weapons, Dave stays calm.

"There's really no reason to be so aggressive, gentlemen," he says. "What is it that you're wanting me to help you with?"

"Have you seen the girl?" the man repeats.

Aquila has her eyes closed now, so she can't see what the men are doing. Are they pinning Dave down? Where are their weapons?

"What does she look like?"

"She's petite. Young. Long hair."

"Sorry, boys. I've not seen her."

How is he so calm? Aquila's heart feels as though it's going to burst out of her chest.

"You're lying!"

Aquila's eyes are still closed so she only hears what happens next: the thwacking sound of a fist connecting with flesh. Gingerly, she opens an eye and sees Dave collapsed on the floor, blood pouring from his temple.

Who are these people? Aquila thinks to herself. *And what do they want to do with me?* Suddenly, Aquila feels like a little girl again: all she wants is for her mum to appear and make everything better.

"GET UP!" one of the men is shouting at Dave now.

Aquila watches as the one with the baseball bat pulls Dave to his feet. Dave stumbles, crashing backwards into the car as the one with the gun punches him again. The others laugh.

This is some kind of game to them, Aquila thinks, incredulous. *What should I do? I can't just let this happen to him… But I don't stand a chance against them myself.*

"Why'd you even bring that bat if you ain't gonna use it, Mike?" the one with the knife says.

"Why are you in such a rush, Steve?" the one with the baseball bat replies. "There's plenty of time for us to all have our turn before we chuck this idiot into the Thames."

This is bad, Aquila thinks, *this is really bad. They're using each other's names in front of us.* She remembers a true-crime book she read when she was younger, which taught her that killers stop trying to conceal their identity when they know their victims won't be alive long enough to go to the police.

"Will you two calm down?" the man with the gun says. "What are we, little boys waiting for our turn on a video game?"

Why isn't Dave saying anything? Aquila thinks, her sense of panic rising. *Is he still conscious?*

"Look, wise guy," the gunman continues, "enough

of this bullshit. Why don't you step over here with my colleague?"

"Why?" Dave replies.

Aquila feels a glimmer of relief to hear that Dave can still speak, but her relief is quickly overwhelmed by terror when she hears the gunman's reply.

"So we can search your car."

Oh my God, oh my God, oh my God. Aquila thinks to herself, shutting her eyes again as though this might protect her from what's about to happen. *What on earth am I going to do?*

"Be my guest, take a look around," Dave replies, to Aquila's horror. "I think you're going to be disappointed though."

Aquila's eyes are still closed but she can hear the gunman leaning into the car from the front passenger seat. Barely a moment later, she opens her eyes at the sound of a scuffle, and sees Dave dragging the gunman back out into the street. Somehow, he has gotten hold of the gun and is holding it to the gunman's temple.

"NOBODY MOVE!" he yells.

Aquila struggles to stay silent as she watches Dave drag the gunman away from the car, his two sidekicks looking warily at Dave, who has one hand clasped over the gunman's mouth and the other clasped around the trigger of the gun.

"If either of you move an inch, I will shoot your boss in the head and you'll be next."

For a moment, there is complete silence.

"Who the hell is this guy, Mike?" one of the men says to the other.

"My name is Dave, and I'm open to negotiation," Dave replies, his voice steady and calm. "But if that negotiation fails, I am equally open to shooting all three of you morons in the head. So choose your next steps carefully."

There is silence again for a few moments, before the man with the baseball bat turns and runs.

"Mike!" the man with the knife calls after him. He hesitates for a moment before turning and running after his 'friend'.

Now it's just Dave, Aquila and the gunman. The only sound that Aquila can hear is her own heartbeat, and the footsteps of the two men receding into the distance.

"Now, I'm going to give you a chance to go after your little friends," Dave says, taking his hand away from the gunman's mouth. "But you'd better be quick about it or –"

Dave's words are cut off by the gunman spinning around and punching Dave, with full force, in the face.

"What did I tell you, you little bastard?" Dave shouts.

Aquila closes her eyes again to shut out the sight of the two men collapsed to the ground. She hears punches; she hears yelling; she hears the sound of a head cracking violently against the road and prays to God that it isn't Dave's.

Aquila has almost given up hope of surviving the night when she hears the car door slam and the engine starting. Moments later, they are tearing away into the night.

"Aquila, are you ok?"

Every inch of Aquila's body floods with relief at the sound of Dave's voice.

"I'm ok," she manages to say, though it's a struggle to get the words out. "But Dave... are you ok? I..."

"I'm fine, Aquila," Dave says as gently as a father comforting his child after a nightmare. "Why don't you come back into the front of the car?"

With great effort, Aquila crawls back into the front passenger seat and puts on her seatbelt, taking in the sight of Dave – blood pouring from his temple; left eye swollen and already starting to blacken.

"But Dave, look at what they've done to you!" Aquila says, reaching out to touch Dave's cheek.

"Don't worry about me, Aquila," Dave says, smiling. "I'm just sorry for the delay in your journey home."

In spite of everything, Aquila can't help but laugh.

How can this man be so calm?

"I think I can forgive you," she says.

"Aquila, you need to tell me why those guys were looking for you."

So Aquila explains everything. Dave sits quietly, his eyes focused on the road, as she reveals every last detail to him. It's so comforting to share her story with this calm man that she barely notices that they have pulled up on the street outside her house.

"Here you are, my lady. Home sweet home."

As much as Aquila feels relief to be safe at last, she feels a tug of sadness at leaving Dave behind.

"I can't just leave you here on your own, bleeding," Aquila says.

"Don't worry about me, sweet girl," Dave says. "I'm in the army. It'll take more than a few silly boys and their little toys to scare me."

"But what about –"

"Aquila, I'll get myself cleaned up. It's just a few scratches. Don't worry about it. What you need is to go inside and get some rest. And no more leaving parties with mysterious strangers. Promise?"

"I promise," Aquila replies. "Thank you for saving my life."

"All in a night's work. Take care of yourself, eh?"

It's only when Dave's car has pulled off into the night, and Aquila is left alone again, that she realises she's forgotten to ask for his number.

*

"Aquila! Aquila! Thank goodness you're home!"

Aquila had been practising a lie about why she was late home from the party – and why she was in such a dishevelled state – but as soon as she walks through the front door, her story goes out the window. Her mother doesn't seem to notice her torn clothes or tear-stained face – there's something more pressing on her mind.

"Aquila, thank goodness you're here! Come

quickly!" her mother says, grabbing her hands and pulling her towards the living room.

"Mother, what is it? You're being hysterical!" Aquila says.

"It's your father! Your father..."

"What's happened, Mum?"

"I need you to call the ambulance, please..." Cristina manages to say before collapsing to the kitchen floor in tears.

"An ambulance? Mum, where is he?"

"Aquila he's collapsed... He was drinking... We were waiting for you... I couldn't stop him..." Tina's words come out in tearful fragments, interspersed with guttural sobs.

"Ok, Mum, listen, don't worry. I'm here. I'll call them. It's ok, Mum, I've got you."

Has some of Dave's strength and calm rubbed off on me? Aquila asks herself, as she dials 999.

"Hello? Operator? I need an ambulance. It's my father."

The operator patiently runs through her list of questions with Aquila. Can he move? No. Can he speak? No. Is anyone with him now? Yes, my Mum. Aquila turns to look at her mother, tearful and frantic, as she tries to reassure her ailing husband. Within a few moments, an ambulance has been arranged and there is nothing for Aquila and Cristina to do but wait. Worry and wait.

The next few minutes feel like hours. Aquila talks to her father, struggling to find the words to comfort him or her mother. Somehow though, she herself remains calm and in control. Perhaps the events of the night so far have made Aquila immune to panic or fear.

Aquila's father's jaw is sagging, and he has started to shiver. His breathing is laboured and starting to slow. *Where are they?* Aquila thinks to herself; she can't help thinking about Dave, and the fact that things would be sorted in an instant, if only he were here to help.

*

It's not until the ambulance arrives – and she sees the urgency with which they manage her father – that Aquila starts to feel any true sense of worry.

"Give us space!" one of the crew barks.

Aquila watches as the team lifts her father onto a stretcher and into the ambulance, frantically arranging tubes and wires, barely taking a moment to acknowledge Aquila or her mother.

"Oh my God, my poor husband," Cristina sobs, to nobody in particular. "Please... Please help him." When nobody responds, she holds onto the arm of one of the paramedics, who shakes her off brusquely.

"Ma'am, please give us the space we need to do our job properly," he says to her, dismissively, before returning his attention to his colleague. "We need to get this man to A&E. Immediately."

The next few minutes are a blur: Cristina crying; paramedics barking instructions; machines bleeping. Before Aquila can blink, she and her mother have been left standing alone on the front porch, the ambulance receding into the distance. The paramedics had refused to let Cristina go in the ambulance, so they have agreed to follow on in a few minutes.

"This is unreal," Aquila says, at last. "If only I hadn't gone to that stupid party."

"Aquila, my love," Cristina says, her voice much calmer now that her husband has gone. "Please don't blame yourself."

"But you were up worrying, if I had just –"

"No," Cristina interrupts, firmly. "Your father may have been worrying about you, but this is about more than a father's worry. That man has been drinking himself to death every single night for the past 20 years. He has no one to blame but himself."

"Oh, Mum," Aquila says, because she can't think of anything else to say. "I just hope he's ok."

"Me too, my girl. Me too."

"Did you have a good time at the party, at least?" Cristina asks, rubbing her daughter's shoulder affectionately.

Aquila hesitates for a moment before responding.

Now really isn't the right time for honesty, she decides.

"Yes, I did thanks," she says, smiling guiltily.

"Well, I'd better start making my way to the hospital."

"Without me? I can't leave you on your own, Mum."

"Aquila, you need rest. Who knows what will happen at the hospital, but I can call you as soon as I know more."

Aquila wants to be there for her father, but the mention of rest makes her realise just how tired she is.

"Well… If you're sure, Mum."

"And Aquila?"

"Yes, Mum?"

"Make sure you lock all the doors and windows. There are some weird people out there."

Aquila kisses her mother on the cheek as they part ways. "Mother, you have no idea how right you are."

CHAPTER EIGHT

"BANG! BANG! BANG!"

Aquila is torn from her sleep by a frantic hammering sound, which brings her lurching into consciousness, terrified, panting, drenched with sweat.

It's him, she thinks, with horror. *Or his men. They've found me.*

BANG! BANG! BANG!

This time, she's awake enough to realise that it isn't a gun firing: it's a knock at the door. But whoever it is, they're knocking with a sense of urgency.

"Aquila! Aquila! Are you in there?"

Relief floods Aquila's heart as she realises that it isn't Donald or his henchmen: it's just Charlotte. Aquila walks to her bedroom window and opens it, leaning out to see her best friend, fresh faced and stylishly dressed in loungewear, a takeaway coffee in each hand.

"Charlotte!" she calls down. "Sorry, I was asleep. Let me come down and let you in."

Aquila throws on an old dressing gown, runs a brush through her hair and rushes downstairs to let her friend in. On her way down, she checks her phone: eight missed calls, a message ('Call me when you get this') and a voicemail from Mum. *Oh, God*, she thinks, *what have I slept through?* She's so distracted by worries for her father that she has briefly forgotten about the events of last night.

"Well, well, well," Charlotte says, as Aquila lets her into the hallway. She raises her eyebrows at Aquila, placing one of the coffees in her hand. "You're alive, then?"

"Alive?" Aquila responds, stalling for time.

"I left you for a few minutes to catch up with my cousins. When I came back, you were gone! Aunt Betty said she saw you talking to some old guy…"

"Oh, I'm sorry Charlotte," Aquila replies. Now isn't the time for telling the truth. "I was just… I took a funny turn and decided to get a taxi home. I tried to find you but… I guess you were talking to your cousins."

Charlotte looks at Aquila suspiciously. "So what about this old guy?"

"Hmm…" Aquila ponders this, guiltily, trying to think of an alibi. Nothing comes to mind, so she decides to distract her friend instead. "I'm not sure who Betty's talking about… But my mind's a bit all over the place. It's Dad…"

"Your Dad? What about him?"

"He's in hospital."

"He's WHAT?"

"Hospital. When I got back from the party, he was in a total state."

"Oh my God, Aquila, why didn't you say? I'm sorry for giving you a hard time about leaving the party, I didn't realise, I…"

"Really, Charlotte, it's ok. I do feel bad that I left when I did."

"Forget about it, really," Charlotte says. "I shouldn't have left you to talk to my cousins."

How different last night would have been if she hadn't, Aquila thought to herself.

"Aquila, let me take you to the hospital," Charlotte says.

"No, really Charlotte, it's fine," Aquila responds. "You should go to college. Don't worry about me. Maybe you could just tell our teachers why I'm not there.

She feels bad, palming her friend off, but Aquila can't handle being around Charlotte right now. What if the truth of last night slips out, or she asks questions that Aquila can't answer? Besides, she needs to focus on her parents for the time being.

"Take care of yourself," Charlotte says, as she climbs back into her car, and Aquila wonders if her friend can feel the words that have gone unspoken between them.

CHAPTER NINE

Donald wakes with such an acute, screaming headache that he has to pull his bedsheets over his head to shut the light out.

I'm still here, at least, he thinks to himself, focusing on taking deep breaths to ease the piercing pain in his temples. Tenderly, he touches his fingers to the source of the pain, and recoils at the sticky, matted blood that he finds there.

Oh, God, he thinks, reaching one arm out of the bed in order to feel around for his phone. *What I wouldn't give for a whiskey and a warm bath now.*

He dials the number and, to his great relief, his friend picks up after only one ring.

"Hello?"

"Jack, is that you?"

"Yes, Donald. It's me."

"Good. Jack, I need you to do something for me."

"Yes, boss, of course. Is there something you need me to sort out?"

The line goes quiet for a moment, and Jack wonders if his boss has hung up.

"Boss? Are you still there? What can I do for you, boss?"

"Jack, listen. I had a young lady at my house last night and she… left. Unexpectedly early. Now… You know the drill. I need you to… clean up the mess."

"Boss, don't worry about a thing. I've got you. Just tell me what happened. Who is this girl and where did you find her?"

Donald opens his mouth to begin the tale, but is cut off by the flashing of red and blue lights, slicing through the bedroom curtains and flooding the bedroom.

"Jack, I'll call you back," Donald says.

Frantically, he rushes to the ensuite to wash his

face. The sink fills with blood as Donald scrubs at the scabby wound on his temple. *What am I going to do?* he thinks. *They've literally got me with blood on my hands.*

In a flash of inspiration, he ties a small towel around his head, as though he's just emerged from washing his hair in the shower. *They don't need to know how short my hair is.* Donald tells himself, positioning the towel to hide his injury, then quickly straightening up the bedroom to hide any sign of last night's struggle. He has just finished making the bed and slipping into his smartest, most expensive dressing robe when the policemen knock at the front door.

"Hello, officers," he says, confidently, as he opens the door to two stern looking men in uniform. "What seems to be the problem?"

CHAPTER TEN

As Aquila sits in the hospital waiting room, she turns the events of last night over and over in her mind. *What would have happened if I hadn't managed to get away from Donald? she asks herself. What would he have done to me? And how stupid was I to swan off in a car with a total stranger, just because he seemed rich and charming? From now on, I need to take better care of myself. No more men… I just need to focus on my studies and looking after my mum and dad.*

Aquila's stream of thought is interrupted by her mother arriving in the waiting room.

"Hello, sweetheart. Would you like a cup of tea from the vending machine?"

Cristina looks totally drained, as though she has no tears left in her to cry.

"That's ok, Mum," Aquila replies, holding her hand out to her mother. "How's Dad doing?"

"Aquila, darling," her mum says, in a voice so gentle that it panics her.

"What, Mum? What is it? Tell me." Aquila can feel her eyes filling with tears with every word.

"My darling Aquila. I know that your father isn't perfect. I know he has his moments... But you know... When we first got together, he had so little confidence in himself..."

Tina's voice is starting to break with the upset, so Aquila strokes her arm to comfort her.

"Mum, it's ok. You don't need to say all this."

"No, Aquila, I do. Because I need you to know... Your father loves you so much. He always wanted a daughter, ever since we first met. Having you changed him from a quiet, uncertain man to a confident, loving father. I can't deny that his drinking got in the way of him being the best parent, at times. But he always did the best he could with what he had... Being your father was the most important thing in the world to him."

This is bad, Aquila thinks, as her mum squeezes her

hand so tightly that it hurts. *Mum never praises Dad. This is bad.*

"I know I give your father a hard time, and I moan a lot," Cristina continues, as though she's read Aquila's mind. "But he's a good man. When you spend all your time with someone, it's easy to forget about the good and to focus entirely on the bad."

"Mum, please. Why are you saying all of this?"

Tina's looks at her daughter with eyes filled with sadness. "Darling, this is it. Your father's time has come. Whether it's a few hours or a few days, I'm not sure, but your dad doesn't have much longer left with us on this earth."

The truth hits Aquila like a tsunami wave: pain washes through her entire body, followed by a rush of numbness. Her throat feels tight; her head throbs and tears begin to flow, unbidden, down her cheeks. *My poor father*, she thinks, feeling totally lost. *My poor dad.*

"Please, Mum," she says, "I need to hear all the details. Don't spare me the truth."

So Cristina explains. Sometimes she has to stop

and cry, but she explains it all. She explains about the tumour that the doctors have found on her father's brain; the cancer that has colonised his lungs and which is now spreading throughout his entire body; that the daily drinking – a habit inherited from his father and grandfather – has finally caught up with him.

"I know it's hard, Aquila, but we have to be brave. We have to be brave for your father."

Her mother collapses onto Aquila's shoulder and weeps. Aquila wraps her arm around her mother and gives her an affectionate squeeze. She wants to be strong for her mother, though it feels as though her entire world is collapsing around her. *He's only 55* years old, she thinks to herself. *How can this be the end of the road for him? Surely he deserves another chance.*

Aquila and her mother sit like this for some time, Aquila rubbing Tina's arm reassuringly and Cristina sobbing softly, helplessly, like a child after waking from a bad nightmare. *Except this nightmare isn't going away,* Aquila thinks. *There's no waking up from this.*

The wind is moaning eerily, causing the tree branches outside to pound menacingly against the windows. It's June, but it sounds as though it's the depths of winter outside the hospital.

"Mum," Aquila says, gently, "let me go and get us both a cup of tea."

As she walks along the corridor, she feels as though she's walking through a dream. *How can so much have happened in only 24 hours?* Aquila wonders. *How can it be that – only a day ago – my biggest worry in the world was what dress to wear to Betty and Paul's party?* Since then, it feels as though Aquila's entire world has been torn into shreds.

"Excuse me?"

Aquila is pulled back to reality by the sound of a stranger. It's a man – looking at her and frowning.

"Can I help you?" Aquila asks. She assumes that this man works at the hospital, but his casual clothes tell a different story.

"I need you to come with me into this side room," the man says, taking Aquila by the arm and gesturing down the corridor.

The hairs on Aquila's arms stand on end and she feels dread building in her stomach.

"Is this about my father?" she asks, her voice tremulous.

"It'll all become clear in a minute, Aquila," the man says. "But you have to come with me."

How does he know my name? Aquila thinks. "Hey!" she says, yanking her arm away firmly. "Tell me what you want!"

"I *am* telling you!" the man says, grabbing onto her arm again. "I want you to come with me into this side room."

Aquila looks around and realises, with a note of panic, that there is no one around that she can ask for help from. The man's grip is fierce and firm, and she decides that there's not much she can do except go along with him. As he guides her along a corridor, she does all she can to stop herself from shaking. Soon, they reach a side room and, after knocking lightly, the strange man opens the door and pulls her inside.

"I'm back," the man says, "and I've got what you

asked for."

"Thank you." The voice that replies is croaky and pained, and muffled by a bandage wound round the entirety of the speaker's head.

"What is going on?" Aquila asks, trying to sound brave and not being entirely successful. "I don't have time for this – my father is unwell."

"Will you shut up?" the strange man snaps, but the bandaged man with the croaky voice raises a hand to silence him.

"Quiet, quiet, please," he says. "This will only take a moment."

"What will only take a moment?" Aquila asks, baffled.

"Chris," says the bandaged man to his aggressive crony. "I need you to sign the papers at the end of my bed. And the girl, too."

"Why?" Aquila asks, as Chris shoves a fountain pen into her shaking hand.

"Just sign here, God damn it," Chris says, thrusting the papers under her nose. "You really don't want to be making this any more complicated than it needs to be."

Aquila hesitates. Maybe it's the craziness of the past 24 hours; maybe it's exhaustion; maybe it's desperation to get back to her mother and to see her father. Whatever it is, Aquila shrugs and signs her name onto the document.

"Did she sign?" the bandaged man asks, his voice tortured.

He does not sound like a healthy man, Aquila thinks.

"Yes. Right. Good," Chris says. "It's done. Now, get out!"

Before she has a chance to think, Chris has opened the door and pushed Aquila out into the corridor, slamming the door shut again behind her.

What am I doing? Aquila thinks to herself, but she barely has time to complete the thought before she bumps into a man in a white doctor's coat, causing his papers to spill onto the floor of the hospital corridor.

"For goodness' sake, watch where you're going!" the doctor mutters, in a voice which strikes Aquila as oddly familiar.

"I'm so sorry, I was away in my own world," Aquila says, squinting to try and see the face of this strangely familiar doctor. "Let me help you with those," she adds, crouching to collect some of the scattered papers.

"No, just... back off!" The doctor snaps back, in a voice so aggressive that it takes Aquila by surprise. "Look, just watch where you're going next time, ok? This is a hospital, you know! People are busy and they don't have time to waste getting tripped up by airheads like you."

"Wow!" Aquila says, practically speechless in the face of this rude doctor. "You're incredibly impolite. I was just trying to help you."

"Well, don't," the doctor replies, and he looks up at last to reveal to Aquila an extremely familiar face.

"Dave!" Aquila gasps.

"Who?" the doctor replies, stony faced. "Look, lady. I'm a doctor but I'm not a psychiatrist... I don't have time to deal with whatever weird episode you seem to be going through right now. I'm not Dave, and I have places to be. Goodbye."

With that, the doctor sweeps his papers up into a pile and hurries off down the corridor.

"Wait! Wait!" Aquila calls after him. "It is you! I know it! I know I was in a bad way but I wouldn't have forgotten the face of the man who saved my life."

"I'm sorry to disappoint you, lady, but you've got the wrong guy. And I really don't have time to stand here listening to your teenage fantasies."

With that, the doctor spins on his heels and walks away, leaving Aquila to reel at the unfriendliness of this stranger, and the bizarre fact of his looking and sounding exactly like her hero but acting like his exact opposite.

Numbly, listlessly, Aquila walks to the vending machine and purchases two cups of tea. She carries them back to the waiting room where she was sitting with her mother less than half an hour ago, but there is no one there.

"Hello?" Aquila calls, tentatively, clutching the two polystyrene cups.

The silence of the corridor is deafening.

*

After pacing frantically up and down the warren-like corridors of the hospital for what feels like an eternity, Aquila finally finds a bored looking nurse sitting at a reception desk, taking a phone call.

"Mmm hmm," the nurse is saying into the phone, clearly uninterested in whatever the person on the other end of the line has to say.

Aquila smiles weakly at the nurse, who raises her eyebrows and looks Aquila up and down appraisingly, not smiling back.

"Go on...." the nurse says into the phone, "I'm listening."

After what seems like an eternity, the nurse hangs up the phone with a click, rearranges some papers on the desk before her and sighs deeply before turning her attention to Aquila.

"How can I help?"

"Please can you help me to find my father? His name is Robert Lawrence... He's 55 years old... He was admitted to A&E last night... My mother and I were in the waiting room together and I just went to get some cups of tea but –"

"Ok, ok," the nurse says, raising a hand to halt Aquila's frenzied speech. "Let's see what I can see."

The nurse turns her attention to the computer screen and begins typing lazily, the sound of her long nails clacking against the keyboard.

"If you don't mind, it's kind of an emergency..." Aquila says, awkwardly, and immediately regrets her decision to speak. The nurse's eyes are daggers which glint viciously and cause Aquila's voice to dry up in her throat.

"Honey, every minute of every day is an emergency in this place. What makes you so special?"

"Sorry," Aquila mutters, and she gazes down at her feet bashfully until the nurse returns her attention to the screen.

"Your father is on Ward 452. Fourth floor. Turn left after the cafe. If you reach the toilets, you've gone too far."

The relief that Aquila feels as she approaches the ward is quickly replaced with panic when she gives her father's name to the nurse at reception on Ward 452.

"You're the daughter?" the nurse asks, her eyes wide, her voice firm.

"Yes," Aquila replies, her voice trembling.

"We've been trying to get hold of you for a while. Your mother's been asking for you. Come with me, they're in Bay Eight."

The nurse turns on her heels and starts walking down the corridor before Aquila has a chance to respond. The briskness of her pace and the lack of reassurance cause the panic to rise in Aquila's throat.

"Here she is," the nurse says into the bay.

"Aquila!" Cristina exclaims, standing and opening her arms wide, as though this reunion has been years in the making.

"Mum! What happened? I was only gone for half an –"

"Never mind, you're here now," Cristina guides Aquila towards the hospital bed where her dad is lying.

Robert's eyes are closed, and various tubes – attached to bleeping machines – are connected to his nose and arms. In his thin hospital gown, he looks incredibly fragile to Aquila. Her mother, too, looks far older than her years, and Aquila notices for the first time the frown lines etched around her eyes; the wiry grey hairs at her temple.

"Mum... No one's told me what's happening. Please," Aquila squeezes Tina's hand, seeing reassurance. "What's happening to Dad?"

Tina's eyes are full of sorrow as she replies. "Your father has had a stroke. For a moment, it looked as though it was going to be the last time we saw him, but the doctors were able to help him and now, thank the heavens, he seems to have stabilised."

"Oh Mum, I'm sorry you had to go through that

alone." Aquila squeezes her mum tightly and kisses her cheek. "I wish I'd never gone for those cups of tea! I love you, Mum. So much."

Aquila feels Cristina soften in her arms at these words.

"I love you too darling. At least we've got each other, eh? And I tell you what… I wouldn't mind that cup of tea now!" Cristina says, smiling for the first time since all of this started.

Aquila glances over at the two polystyrene cups, sitting forlornly on the table at the side of Robert's bed, the tea stone cold.

"Maybe I should go and get some fresh ones," Aquila suggests, smiling.

"I tell you what, love. You stay here with your dad. I could do with a leg stretch. I won't be long, ok?"

"Take all the time you need, Mum."

With Cristina gone, Aquila sits at Robert's side and takes his limp hand in hers, giving it a gentle squeeze. *I miss you, Dad, so much*, she thinks. *I know you're not perfect, but who of us is? I know you love me unconditionally. I know I'll always be your little girl.* Aquila's heart bursts with love for her father as they sit together, hand in hand, and she thinks of the cruelty of his addiction to alcohol, which has taken so much from him: his career; his health; his happiness. *I forgive you, Dad, for drinking like you did. I love you so much. Just… please don't leave Mum and me. We'll be lost without you, Dad, please…"*

Tears are streaming down Aquila's face now, and she rests her head on her father's shoulder. Lying here like this, Aquila feels like a little girl again, and she feels her whole relationship with her father flashing before her eyes.

"Dad, do you remember when I was four years old and I lost my favourite teddy, Cindy?" She asks, though she knows he can't reply. *Maybe he can hear me though*, she thinks. For now, that 'maybe' is enough. "I was only a little girl but I still remember the advice you gave to me that day. You said 'Aquila, don't give up. You will find Cindy eventually. Whatever happens in life, so long as you keep fighting and never give up, so long as you keep focusing on finding a solution to your problem, you will always find light at the end of the tunnel. So don't give up, and I promise we will find Cindy eventually.' Well, Dad. It took us three days – and three days feels excruciating when you're four years old – but we found her! Our dog, Barney, had played with her and had buried her in the next door neighbour's garden. Our neighbour found her – do you remember? She was covered in mud and a little worse for wear, but she was still intact, and you were right all along. We just had to not give up... And we found her. So that's what you need to do now, Dad, ok? You need to fight for your life. Don't give up! Because there's still light at the end of the tunnel. There's still hope."

The tears are flowing freely down Aquila's cheeks now, and she can hardly believe it when she feels her father's hand twitch in hers.

"Dad?" she cries, delightedly. "Did you just squeeze my hand?"

Robert's face remains still and unmoved, but Aquila's heart leaps for joy when she feels her father's hand gently squeeze hers again.

"Dad, I'm here, ok? I'm here and I love you so much! Please don't leave us. I know I've not been the perfect daughter... I wish I could have the chance to make it up to you now... For all the times I shouted at you or snapped at you when I was a teenager... Oh, Dad. I wish I could talk to you! I feel like I've grown up so much over the last few days and I just wish that I could talk to you about it all! I feel better about it already, just holding your hand and knowing you're here. Dad, you have to get better so that I can look after you like you've always looked after me... Please, Dad. Please keep fighting. You still have a big place in this world. You are too young to leave us... Mum and I couldn't bear it if you weren't around anymore..."

Aquila is so immersed in her thoughts and words that she doesn't even notice as her father opens his eyes and looks at her, lovingly, for a few peaceful seconds before the machine begins to bleep.

"Nurse! Nurse!" Aquila yells, as though she has just discovered a fire. "Please come quickly! My father needs your help!"

By the time she looks into her father's face, searching for signs of life, Robert's eyes are already closed.

The next few minutes pass in a blur of frenzied activity. Doctors and nurses come in and out of the bay, hurrying Aquila out of the room and talking to each other in unfamiliar, technical language that

Aquila can make no sense of. The machine continues with its droning bleep, and Aquila can do nothing but listen, helplessly, and pray for her mother's return.

Aquila is pacing up and down the corridor when Cristina returns to the ward, two fresh cups of tea in hand.

"Aquila?" she says, her face filling with panic at the sight of her frantic daughter.

"Mum, it's Dad. He's gotten worse."

"Oh my God, oh my God…" Cristina hurries past Aquila, thrusting the cups of tea into her daughter's hands and running into the bay.

*

Aquila is in the waiting room again. It feels as though she has been in this hospital for a lifetime, alternating between the waiting room and the ward. Her heart seems to be stuck on an endlessly looping roller coaster of emotions: boredom; panic; heartbreak.

"Excuse me."

Aquila is pulled from her dark thoughts and looks up to see a tall, dark, handsome doctor with charming eyes and a white coat, gazing down at her. It takes her a moment to realise that it's the same unfriendly doctor she bumped into earlier.

"Hello again, Dave. Or not Dave," she says.

"Look, lady. What's your name?" the doctor asks, brusquely.

"Aquila."

"Well, Aquila, I'm sorry to disappoint you... But whoever it is that you think I am... It's not me. Ok?"

"Why do you keep denying it?" Aquila asks, frustration building in her chest. After everything she's been through over the last few days, she doesn't have time for this guy's mind games. "I know who you are. All I wanted was to say thank you for what you did for me, but if you don't want to accept my thanks then that's fine. I don't care."

Aquila stands and turns to walk away.

"My name's Richard," the man calls after her.

What is this guy's problem? Aquila thinks to herself.

"Aquila!" Tina's anguished voice echoes through the corridor, sending a chill down Aquila's spine.

"Yes, Mum?"

Tina's eyes are brimming with tears as her eyes meet her daughter's. "It's time."

*

Aquila finds her father with his eyes closed, the room quieter and calmer than it was the last few times she entered it. There's only one doctor here now; no one is shouting commands anymore, and no machines are bleeping.

"Dad!" Aquila cries, racing towards her father's bedside.

To her immense surprise, Robert opens his eyes ever so slightly and parts his lips to breathe his daughter's name. "Aquila. Darling," he manages to whisper, though the effort of it seems to take everything he has.

"Dad," Aquila repeats, taking her father's hand

in hers. "I love you so much. Please don't leave me, please."

"My little girl," Robert replies, in a croaky whisper. "I'll never leave you. Remember that. I'll always be here. I love you so much. Please... Don't forget to look after your mother for me."

Aquila can't think of anything to say so, instead, she embraces him tightly and sobs.

"I'm sorry..." Robert continues, each word seeming to cost him more. "I'm sorry that I wasn't the father you deserved."

"Dad, no, stop it," Aquila says, sitting up and looking her father squarely in the eye. "You have nothing to apologise for. You're the most wonderful father I could have ever asked for."

Aquila stares into her father's eyes with fierce conviction. He looks back, seemingly soothed by her words, before closing his eyelids slowly and exhaling a deep, peaceful breath.

Tina, who has been standing in the doorway and watching her daughter, rushes forward now and joins

Robert and Aquila in a long embrace. Both Cristina and Aquila are sobbing loudly, and when they finally release their hug, Robert is gone.

"Ladies, I am so sorry for your loss," says the doctor who has been standing and waiting patiently behind them. "Please, take as much time as you need. If you'd like me to escort you to the hospital chapel so that you can light a candle and say a prayer for your father, just let me know."

For Aquila, holding the hand of her dead father, the whole of reality is turning upside down. Yet somehow, she is able to discern the voice of the doctor as the voice of Dave. Or Richard. Or whoever this strange man claims to be.

"You," Aquila says, turning to face him.

"I just want to help in any way I can," the man says, with a smile that Aquila interprets as a smirk.

"My father has –" Aquila is about to tell the mysterious doctor exactly what she thinks of him when the soft, plaintive voice of her mother cuts her short.

"Go with him, Aquila. Light a candle for your father. I'd like some time alone with my husband, if you don't mind."

*

Doctor Richard and Aquila are only a little way along the corridor when the commotion starts. There's a rising hubbub emerging from the double doors behind them, and all kinds of people in uniform are starting to run in the direction of Robert's ward.

"What's going on?" Richard manages to ask one of them, but they barely stop to acknowledge him.

"Ward 452! Bay 8!" They call back over their shoulder, frantically.

"Dad?" Aquila says, confused. "Why are they –"

But Richard is already running back towards the ward. "Wait here for me!" he calls back to Aquila. "I'll find out what's going on!"

Aquila does as Richard says and waits on the corridor for what feels like an eternity, the sounds of shouting and barked commands continuing to pour

AQUILA: THE ADVENTURES OF A YOUNG GIRL

out of Robert's ward. *Why would my father's passing cause this much chaos?* she thinks. *Surely, this is no big deal to them? It's just like that nurse said to me earlier... Every day is an emergency in this place...*

Eventually, Richard returns. His pace is slow and his eyes are sorrowful and downcast.

"What is it?" Aquila asks, panicked.

"Aquila..." Richard replies, his voice trailing off. "Aquila, I'm so sorry."

Then, to Aquila's surprise, Richard pulls her into a tight embrace. The smell of expensive aftershave fills Aquila's nostrils as Richard presses her closely to him.

"What is it?" Aquila asks, her voice muffled by the collar of Richard's white coat.

When Richard finally answers, Aquila's blood runs cold.

"It's your mother."

CHAPTER ELEVEN

The next day, Aquila sits alone in her family kitchen, at the same table where – only a few days ago – her parents had sat and bickered about wine and bills.

And now I'm all alone, she thinks.

The cupboards are still full of food purchased by her mother, with plans to make meals that, now, she would never eat. Her father's newspaper is still lying on the counter, with a crossword destined to be half finished forever.

How could they do this to me? Aquila thinks. *How can they leave me to deal with all of this by myself?*

Aquila puts her head in her hands and sobs. Deep, guttural sobs. It's all she can do to squash down the memories of yesterday, but she can't bear to contemplate them now. *It all happened so fast,* Richard had said. *There was nothing anyone could have done.*

She won't have felt any pain, he had said. Aquila repeats this to herself, rocking back and forth in her chair, sobbing. *She won't have felt any pain. She won't have felt any pain.*

The sound of the doorbell brings Aquila back to reality. Without so much as wiping her eyes, she stumbles to the front door and opens it.

"Hi, Aquila."

The man standing in front of her is smartly dressed in expensive looking jeans and a navy cashmere sweater. His chocolate brown hair is neatly slicked back and there's a bouquet of red roses in his hand.

"Richard," she says, softly. She's still convinced that this man is Dave, her hero, but the distinct scent of this man's aftershave tells her that it's the doctor she met yesterday. The doctor who held her in his arms only a day ago, and told her that her mother had taken her own life.

"I know this isn't exactly professional," he says, his voice more sheepish than yesterday. "But I wanted to make sure you were ok."

"Oh. Well... Thanks. I'm not ok. But thanks."

"Well, yes... I... I brought that on myself, I guess."

"Would you like to come in for a cup of tea?" Aquila asks, knowing that her mother would tell her to stop being so rude to their guest, if she were here.

Richard beams warmly. "A coffee would be great."

In the kitchen, Aquila boils the kettle and scoops coffee granules into mugs. As she does so, she realises that she's never actually made a cup of coffee before. Her mother would normally do it for her.

"I hope that's strong enough for you," she says, as she passes Richard a worryingly pale drink. There are flecks of coffee floating on the surface, which never seemed to happen with Mum's coffees. "Sorry doctor, you're actually my first customer. Mum... Mum always used to do this stuff for me."

Aquila turns away from Richard and begins arranging the roses in a vase, so that he won't see the fresh tears rolling down her cheeks.

"You don't need to hide your tears from me," Richard

says, tenderly. "And you don't need to call me doctor. Not in your own home and not on your day off."

"Ok," Aquila says, turning to face him. "So, seeing as you are in my home... And seeing as you know everything I've been through over the last day... I'm going to ask you one more time. Are you or are you not the man that saved me the other night? The man who told me his name was Dave?"

Richard smiles a sad smile and shakes his head. "I'm sorry, Aquila. I don't know who this man is that you met, and I don't know what he saved you from, but it wasn't me. I swear on my life. On God."

"But it just... I don't...."

"Think about it," Richard says, taking Aquila's hand in his. "Why would I lie to you about it? A beautiful girl comes up to me and tells me I'm the hero that saved her life. Why would I want to lie about that?"

Aquila joins Richard at the kitchen table and passes him the badly made cup of coffee.

"If you say so," she says, feeling as baffled as ever.

"Look, Aquila, there is actually another reason I'm here," Richard says, reaching into his bag and pulling out a thick envelope. "There's some paperwork that you need to fill out after... after everything that happened yesterday. You know, stuff to do with funerals, insurance and so on..."

"Oh God," Aquila says, dropping her head into her hands. "I've just no idea where to begin with any of that. I mean I think I'm still in a state of shock... I've not even spoken to my college..."

"Really, Aquila, it's ok. No one's expecting you to be on top of all of this stuff. That's why I volunteered to drop it over – I figured you could probably do with some support. And besides, I had some making up to do. I was pretty unfriendly to you yesterday, and that was the last thing you needed."

"Well, thank you."

"You're welcome... And actually, there was one strange thing about all those documents."

"Oh?"

"Yeah. Some guy – a guy who claimed to know you

really well – handed in something to pass on to you. He said you'd know what it was about…"

Aquila can't think of a simple explanation to give Richard, so she decides to change the subject instead.

"Richard, do you think you'd be able to help me out with some of this stuff? I know you're probably a very busy man but… maybe I could make you another coffee?"

"Hey, it couldn't be worse than the first one, could it?" Richard replies, flashing Aquila a mischievous smile.

"Hey!" Aquila exclaims, patting Richard lightly on his arm and noticing the firmness of the muscle beneath his jumper. "It was my first time!"

"Well, I suppose I could be persuaded to help you out… And to give you a second chance."

"I think you're the one that needs a second chance," Aquila retorts, standing to turn the kettle on again, "after that terrible first impression you made yesterday."

"That's fair. I was a bit of a jerk. Ok, let me try again.

Please, beautiful lady that stands before me. Would you be so kind as to provide me with a cup of coffee so that I might have the energy to spend my day-off filling out paperwork for you?"

For the first time since the chaos of the day before, Aquila laughs. As she does so, she reveals her perfectly white teeth to Doctor Richard, and the soft dimples that form when she smiles. She watches him watching her, and sees something change in his eyes as he studies her.

"Well, at least I made you smile today. It was worth coming over just for that."

"I'm glad you came," Aquila replies.

For a moment, both of them are silent, staring into each other's eyes. Aquila can feel the tension building between them, filling the room, weighing down on her. The intensity that had existed between the two of them yesterday – that had manifested as anger and frustration – is still here now. Only now, it feels like desire.

Without turning away his gaze, Richard stands. Aquila feels a desperate yearning to be held by him, for him to wrap his strong arms around her, for him to press her into his muscular chest. As he steps towards her, her heart starts to race.

"Maybe you need me to show you how it works."

"I do?"

Richard takes a step towards Aquila, and her heart seems to race even faster.

"Yeah, I mean, if it's your first time and you're not really sure what you're doing. You need someone with experience to take you through it, step by step."

Richard takes another step forward. They're barely a metre apart now, and the intensity of his gaze seems to prickle Aquila with heat. She can hardly gather her words enough to reply.

"Oh?"

"Because a girl like you? With all that you've got going on? With the right experience, you could be making world-class cups of coffee."

Aquila giggles and Richard smiles back at her, taking both of her hands in his and drawing her towards him.

"If I'd have seen how beautiful you were when you first spoke to me yesterday," he says, raising one hand to the small of Aquila's back and the other to cup her face, "I'd have pretended to be this Dave that you seem to love so much. I'd have said anything to be the man that got to kiss these lips."

"I don't want you to be Dave," Aquila replies, breathlessly, as the doctor grazes his thumb lightly against her bottom lip. "I want you to be Richard."

As soon as she whispers his name, Richard takes Aquila's face in both of his hands and presses his lips against hers. They kiss hungrily, passionately, his hands roving frantically all over her body, every touch feeling like an electric shock to Aquila. She can tell by the way that he is biting her neck that he wants her as desperately as she wants him. When he suddenly lifts her into his arms and carries her up the stairs to the bedroom, Aquila knows that she is powerless to say no to him.

CHAPTER TWELVE

"I should go," Richard says, brushing a hair out of Aquila's eyes as they lay side by side, basking in the post-coital glow. "I've got a lot of stuff to sort out before work tomorrow."

"But what about the paperwork?" Aquila replies.

"I guess I'll have to come back again," Richard says with a smile, kissing Aquila tenderly before getting out of bed and beginning to get dressed.

Once Richard has gone, the yawning silence of Aquila's house creeps back in. The quiet, lifeless rooms are oppressive in their emptiness, and Aquila's mind begins to flood with memories of her parents, of the events of the past few days. She decides to tidy the house from top to bottom, and spends the next few hours scrubbing and polishing every inch of the house, straightening cushions and washing sheets until the whole place smells fresh and feels as spotless and orderly as a five-star hotel.

That's better. She thinks. *A fresh start.*

Aquila turns to the brown envelope of paperwork on the freshly polished kitchen table and considers working through them. *You're an adult, Aquila. You don't need some random guy to help you with this stuff. You're responsible for yourself now.*

Still, the idea of the paperwork makes Aquila's brain hurt. She can't face it just yet. She decides to call someone instead.

"Hello?"

Aquila practically bursts into tears at the sound of her favourite teacher's warm voice.

"Diane!" she exclaims. "It's me! Aquila."

"Aquila, my love! How are you doing? We've missed you in class!"

"You have?" Aquila takes the phone to the living room and collapses into the sofa, cuddling one of the freshly plumped cushions.

"Of course! I've got to say, I was worried about you!

Charlotte mentioned that you wouldn't be in for a while but she told me it was down to personal reasons."

At the phrase 'personal reasons', Aquila starts to cry. The gentleness of her teacher's voice always makes her feel safe, and now it draws out all the pain and hurt that she has been trying to squash down.

"Aquila? Oh, Aquila, honey, why don't you tell me what's wrong?"

So Aquila tells Diane everything. Her teacher is silent and attentive as, through heavy bouts of sobbing, Aquila tells her about her mother and father.

"Oh, Aquila," she says, when the tale is finally complete. "I don't even know where to start. I mean, don't worry about college, for one thing. I'll talk to the staff, ok? You just take all the time you need."

"Thanks, Diane."

"Who's helping you sort out all the practical stuff? Have you got any aunts or uncles, or…?"

"No. It's kind of… Just me. All on my own. To be honest, I don't even know how I'm going to pay for it.

We aren't exactly a wealthy family..."

"Look, Aquila, why don't you come over to my house tomorrow and we can go through all that stuff? You shouldn't be worrying about money or paperwork at a time like this. I'll help you get it all started."

"Really, Diane? I'd appreciate that so much."

"Hey, of course! I mean what are teachers for, eh?"

"You're more than just a teacher Diane. You're my friend."

"Well I'm very glad to hear it."

*

As she boards the bus the next morning, the envelope of paperwork tucked into her backpack, Aquila feels a glimmer of optimism in her heart. The sky is blue, the sun is shining and things don't feel quite as bad as they did yesterday morning. She still has the delicious memory of Richard's visit to enjoy and reflect on, though – just like the rest of the bizarre events of the last few days – it feels almost like it occurred in a dream. *Perhaps it was a dream,* she thinks. *Perhaps that's*

AQUILA: THE ADVENTURES OF A YOUNG GIRL

why I haven't heard from him since.

"Good morning!" she says, brightly, to the bus driver, flashing her student card and swiping up her ticket. As she tucks it into her jean pocket, she scans the bus for an empty seat and stops dead at the sight of a particularly familiar face.

"Oh my God, it's you," she says, stepping towards the handsome man.

The man is distracted by his phone, and startles at the sight of Aquila.

"Aquila!" he says. "It's you!"

"May I join you?" she asks, grabbing onto a handrail as the bus lurches to life.

"Be my guest," the handsome man replies.

As Aquila slides into the seat next to him, she reflects on the uncanny likeness of his voice as well as his face. *They're identical,* she thinks to herself. *There's no denying it.* If it wasn't for the distinct smell of his aftershave, they'd be utterly indistinguishable.

"So Dave," she asks, flirtatiously, "what's a man with his own perfectly good vehicle doing catching the bus?"

Dave laughs, and Aquila notices that his face is warmer than Richard's. While Richard's eyes are fierce and calculating, Dave's are warm and kind.

"Sometimes I like to let other people do the work for me," he says, grinning. "What about you? What's a princess like yourself doing riding with the peasants? Shouldn't you be waving down random drivers and getting them to do your dirty work for them?"

"Touché," Aquila says, with a laugh. "Listen, Dave. There's something I need to ask you about."

Right there and then, on the bus to Diane's house, Aquila confesses to Dave what happened a day earlier. Dave's face is unreadable as she explains her story to him, but when she finishes, he nods calmly.

"It sounds like you met my twin," he says at last.

"You have a twin?"

"I do."

"But… why wouldn't he tell me about you? I kept asking and asking about you…" Aquila says, blushing at her own admission.

"Maybe he doesn't know about me. We were both adopted… by different parents. My parents told me about him when I was a kid, and I looked him up to see what he's doing. He's a doctor, right? Rich family."

"Right," Aquila says, thinking back to Richard's expensive aftershave, the Rolex watch on his wrist, the cashmere jumper. There was no denying that Richard was a man with money.

"In the end, I decided against getting in touch. I don't know… I guess I just thought we seemed too different. I didn't want to risk us not getting on."

"That seems fair. I guess I don't know enough about you to say whether you're different," Aquila replies. "But if I'm honest… I don't think anything would have happened with your twin if… if part of me hadn't believed that it was you. And now that I know that it wasn't…"

To her surprise, tears spring up in Aquila's eyes.

"Sorry, Dave. It's just... it's been a crazy few days. And I'm just really grateful for what you did for me the other night."

Suddenly, Aquila notices that she has missed her stop.

"Oh no! I need to go!" she says to Dave. "That was my stop!"

Dave laughs. "Honestly? Mine was a little while ago too. I just didn't want to stop talking to you."

Aquila blushes. "You know, Dave. I really wish that it was you – not your twin – who came over to my house yesterday."

"Why waste your time on wishing when I can make it your reality?" Dave says with a grin. He takes his phone out of his pocket and hands it to Aquila. "Give me your number and I'll come over as soon as you're ready."

*

That evening, Aquila returns to her spotlessly clean house with a full heart and a mind at peace. Over endless cups of tea and plates of biscuits, Diane has helped her to work through the practical details relating to her parents. Guiltily, she realises that her mind has been more fixated on thoughts of Dave and Richard than her parents, and she takes out her phone to see if either of them have been in touch.

Nothing. Nothing except for a message from Diane checking that she made it home safely and a message from Charlotte inviting herself round after college the next day. She replies to both, makes herself a herbal tea, curls up on the sofa and dials Dave's number.

"Hello?"

"I was very disappointed to get home and realise that you'd not been in touch," she says, playfully. "It's been at least three hours since I saw you."

"And have you managed to avoid throwing yourself at any of my lookalikes in that time?" Dave asks, innocently.

"Hey!" Aquila replies. "That's not fair!"

"Oh, it isn't? Well is it fair that you've more or less seen me naked, and I've got nothing in return?" Dave retorts. "That feels unfair to me!"

"Look, let's not talk about your lookalike, Dave. I want to talk about you."

In the hour or so that follows, Dave and Aquila talk. They talk and talk and talk, until the sun has gone down and Aquila's cup of tea has gone cold in her hand. She tells Dave all of her secrets and, in return, Dave tells her all of his. He tells her about his career in the army, about the difficulty of balancing those experiences with a normal life. He tells her about his life now – a simple routine of pottering in his garage, going to the gym and walking his dog.

"It's taken me a while to get here, but life is good now. I've got a good job, a good home. I've even started counselling. It's a good life. All that's left, I suppose, is finding someone to share it with."

"Dave, you're such a wonderful person," Aquila says. "I wish that it was you that had come over the other day. That it was you that I went to bed with."

Dave pauses and sighs deeply before replying.

"Look, Aquila. So do I. Any man would say the same if he came across a beautiful girl like you. But you've got to follow your heart."

"Dave, that's what I'm trying to say to you. I –"

"Listen. There's clearly something between you and Richard. Besides, he's a doctor with rich parents. He could provide for you in a way that I could never hope to. Think about this carefully, because I don't want to get involved until you know exactly what you want. Ok?"

"Ok." Aquila replies, but tears are pricking in her eyes.

They say their goodbyes and Aquila decides to head upstairs to bed, alone. No one to say goodnight to, no one to promise you'll 'see them in the morning'. *This is how it is, now.* Aquila thinks. *This is life.* As she turns out the lights downstairs and goes to climb the stairs, she notices something. It's the other envelope Richard gave to her: the one from the man who said she'd know what it was all about. For now though, she's too tired to read it over. *Tomorrow, maybe,* she thinks, and walks up the stairs to her bedroom, where her pillow still smells of Richard's aftershave. In spite of her confused feelings towards Dave, the smell of Richard comforts her, and she breathes it in deeply as she drifts off to sleep.

CHAPTER THIRTEEN

Aquila wakes to the sound of the phone ringing. Groggily, her eyes too heavy to open, she answers.

"Hello?"

"I've just finished a night shift and I'm really in the mood for breakfast in bed. Fancy it?"

Aquila grins. "Whose bed?"

"Yours. You don't even have to move. Just say the word and I'm there."

"Ok. What's the word?"

"That's all I needed to hear."

The phone goes dead and Aquila realises that Richard has hung up. Still half asleep, she gets out of bed and heads to the bathroom, thinking that she should probably freshen up before her lover arrives.

She washes her face, combs her hair and brushes her teeth before changing her outfit. Deciding that her baggy, tea-stained polka dot pyjamas don't quite fit the bill, she tosses them into the laundry and scours her wardrobe for an upgrade. Finally, she decides on a silk nightie – rose pink and trimmed with delicate lace – with a matching silk dressing gown. She slips them on, along with a pair of fluffy slippers the colour of candyfloss, and pads downstairs.

There, on the side, is the envelope again. She reaches for it and is about to pull out the contents when the doorbell rings. Taking a deep breath and allowing a gentle, easy-going smile to fall across her face, she opens the door.

"Good morning, princess."

Richard may have been working all night but he looks impeccable as ever. He's wearing hospital scrubs, leaving his tanned arms on show, and he's holding a brown paper bag in each hand.

"Good morning," Aquila replies, with a smile.

"I brought croissants, orange juice, grapes and coffee. I figured we should probably leave the coffee to the experts, this time, eh?"

"How was your shift?" Aquila asks.

Richard doesn't answer. Instead, he steps into the hallway and drops the brown paper bags down onto the side table before sweeping Aquila into his arms and kissing her.

He looks as good as ever. He smells as good as ever. But this time, when Richard kisses her, Aquila feels nothing.

"Is everything ok?" Richard asks, nuzzling into her neck as he speaks. "I've been dreaming of this ever since I left your bed."

"Richard... Maybe we should talk."

After Aquila has explained everything, she and Richard sit in silence for a while, sipping their coffees.

"The thing I don't understand," Aquila says, eventually, "is why you lied to me. Why didn't you tell me you had a twin? What did you have to gain from keeping it a secret? You made me feel like I was going insane, on what was already the worst day of my life."

"I'm sorry, Aquila. I really am. I wish I hadn't lied to you. But you've got to see it from my point of view. I mean… Do you really think I want to be reminded that I'm related to that loser?"

Aquila's eyes widen at this unexpected insult. "Loser?"

"Yeah! I mean, I've been through a lot to get to where I am in life. I'm not exactly desperate to connect myself to that homeless, unemployed waste of space."

"Richard, you have no idea what you're talking about."

The steely tone to Aquila's voice surprises even her.

"Oh, don't I?"

"No, you don't. Your twin is a hero. Not only is he *not* homeless and *not* unemployed… He fought for his country. He's a true gentleman, and he didn't think twice about helping me when I needed him. Dave has a heart of gold, and no amount of money or fancy titles can compare to that."

Richard stares at Aquila, his eyes wide. It has been a

AQUILA: THE ADVENTURES OF A YOUNG GIRL

long time since anyone spoke down to him like this, let alone a silly young girl.

"Wow," he says, at last. "How did you find all of this out? Presumably you rolled straight out of bed with me and into his... Is that right? I hope he's paying you. At least one of us ought to."

Aquila stands up and slaps Richard round the face, hard, before she has time to think twice about the decision.

"Fine," Richard says, standing up and walking towards the front door. "Forget it. You're not worthy of my time, anyway. You're lucky I made the effort that I did for a useless little kid like you. You might be pretty but that's really all you have going for you, Aquila. Maybe you'd be better off with that homeless waste of space, Dave."

Richard is out of the door before Aquila has time to so much as blink. She stands for a moment in the hallway, stunned into silence, before laughing at the ridiculousness of her situation. A week ago, she was an innocent college girl with two argumentative but loving parents and a best friend who got excited about parties. Now, she's a rape survivor and an orphan, trapped in a love triangle with estranged identical twins. *What else could possibly happen to make my life any weirder?* she wonders, as her eyes land on the unopened brown envelope.

Still wearing her sexy lingerie, Aquila sits down on the wooden floor of the hallway and tears open the envelope. Inside, there are various legal documents and a handwritten letter. The documents are packed with technical jargon and the words all start to blur together, but certain phrases leap out and begin to build an impression in her mind. *Sole ownership. Seven-bedroom property. £500,000 in cash. Tax free gift.*

Aquila's mind is reeling, hardly daring to believe what she is reading, as she turns to the handwritten letter.

Dear Aquila,

I am writing this letter to tell you that I am sorry. I'm sorry that I forced myself upon you, and for hurting you. Alcohol is the devil... or, rather, I become the devil when alcohol passes my lips.

The truth is, I won't be around for much longer. Please

don't think that I'm trying to elicit your forgiveness via a sob story, but I was diagnosed with cancer some time ago now, and the prognosis leaves little room for doubt.

With that in mind, I wish to offer you compensation of sorts. Please find enclosed in this envelope the documents which confer onto you the legal rights to possession of a property in the Suffolk countryside – just a little weekend bolthole of mine which I hope you will find amply comfortable – and some pocket money to ensure that you're comfortable until you're on your feet.

By the time you read this, I will be gone. So let me part by saying this: I hope, Aquila, that you can forgive this old and dying man for his temporary loss of sanity in the presence of true beauty.

All my love,

Donald

*

For a moment, Aquila feels dizzy; her brain fizzes as though it has been filled with Coca-Cola. She sits like this for five, maybe ten, minutes before picking up the phone.

"Hello?"

"Charlotte? Can you come over? It's urgent."

"I'll be there in ten minutes."

*

By the time Charlotte arrives, ten minutes later, Aquila has changed into some baggy jeans and an old jumper of her mother's, has called Diane to tell her the good news, and has prepared tea and biscuits for her and Charlotte to share at the kitchen table. It feels like a somewhat formal arrangement, but Aquila feels strangely nervous. Although it has been less than a week since she saw Charlotte, the whole world seems to have turned upside down in that time.

The doorbell rings and, when Aquila opens the front door, she can see in Charlotte's eyes that she's feeling nervous too. How can they be feeling like this, after having shared their whole lives together? First crushes, first kisses, first periods, first parties. Nothing, surely, could come between them after all these years.

"Hi, Charlotte."

"Hello, Aquila."

They stand for a moment in the doorway, awkwardly silent, before Charlotte lunges forward into Aquila's arms. To her surprise, Aquila realises that her best friend is sobbing.

"Aquila, I'm so sorry about your parents. I can't believe it."

A pang of shame shoots through Aquila as she realises that this is why Charlotte is crying. For Aquila, her parents' deaths are just one unbelievable element of an unimaginably dramatic week. The hug relaxes her, though, reminding her that nothing in the world could break the bond between her and her best friend.

"Will you come inside, Charlotte? There's something I need to tell you."

Aquila explains everything to her friend. She tells her about Donald, about running away from his clutches and into the safety of Dave's car. She tells her about the altercation with the gunmen, and Dave's heroic response. She tells her about her experience in the hospital with her parents, and about Richard. Finally, she tells her about the mysterious bandaged man in the hospital, placing the letter on the table so that Charlotte can read it with her own eyes. She talks and talks and talks, until there is nothing left to say. When, at last, her story is complete, Charlotte's jaw has dropped to the floor.

"Aquila... I don't know where to begin. It's like... It's like I saw you less than a week ago when you were a girl and now... You're a woman."

Aquila laughs. "I guess you're right."

"So much for the Young Aquila!"

Aquila laughs. "I guess I need a new nickname. It's about time, eh?"

"Right. How about Aquila, Duchess of Sussex? I mean this house sounds HUGE!" Charlotte says, gesturing to the letter in front of them.

Aquila laughs again. "I think 'Duchess' might be a step too far," she says, with a grin. "But it's a good start." Aquila takes Charlotte's hands in hers and squeezes them tightly. "You're my best friend, Charlotte, in the whole world. Only you could make me laugh like this... After everything that has happened to me this week."

Charlotte smiles back. "You're my best friend, too, Aquila. I'm sorry I haven't been here for you. In fact, I'm just sorry in general. But I'm here now, ok? I promise. No more dealing with this on your own."

*

The sun is gone and the sky is full of stars by the time Charlotte leaves. She gives Aquila a huge hug as she does, promising to help her with the practical details of funeral arranging and house purchasing. As Aquila closes the door behind her best friend, her heart feels fuller than it has all week.

However, not long after Charlotte's departure, Aquila finds herself thinking about Dave. *I wish he was here with me now,* she thinks to herself, as she changes into her pyjamas and curls up on the sofa with a cup of herbal tea, remembering the conversation that they'd shared in this spot the night before. *I really miss him. Maybe I should call him again.* Instead, she puts the thought out of her mind and decides to get an early night. *After all,* she thinks, *I've got a big day at the bank tomorrow.*

CHAPTER FOURTEEN

The next day, as Aquila steps out of Barclays Bank, her status as a wealthy property owner confirmed, she can hardly believe how easily the teller agreed to handing over Donald's fortune. That morning, she had dressed in her smartest outfit – a sleek Chanel shift dress which had nestled at the back of her mother's wardrobe for decades, paired with a simple pair of black Louboutin heels, a black clutch and some oversized black shades, breathing life into the funereal ensemble with a swipe of flame red lipstick and a spritz of her mother's Black Opium perfume. Aquila had agonised over the outfit, wanting to seem chic, sophisticated and rich, as though staking her claim to a fortune were an everyday occurrence for her. She had also wanted, however, to seem sombre. *I can't look too excited about this,* she'd told her reflection in the mirror that morning, smoothing down the hem of her mother's dress. *If they don't believe that I'm grieving Donald, they might get suspicious.*

But the whole thing had been shockingly easy. Aquila had arrived for her appointment just before

11 a.m., and by midday she was stepping back out onto the street, the documents signed and the money transferred, as the official heir to Somersby Manor – a gorgeous, expansive, thatched cottage in the chocolate box village of Cavendish, Sussex.

She's about to hail a taxi home – after all, why not splash the cash, now that she's rich? – when a hand taps her on the shoulder, causing her to practically jump out of her skin.

"Woah, sorry to surprise you, Aquila," says Dave, looking bashful.

"Oh, hello again!" she says, shyly.

"Aquila, I… I might have been a little rash when I said that you should see where things go with Richard," Dave says.

"Oh?"

"Yeah. I mean… as soon as I got home, I realised what a huge mistake I'd made. I was an idiot to think I could give you over to him so easily. And besides, my brother… He might be rich and have a good job… but he's not a nice guy. He's not going to take care of you like... like I would. If you gave me the chance."

Aquila beams at this, and feels her whole body fill with warmth.

"Let me get this straight," she says, struggling to conceal her grin. "You're a man who keeps his cool when there's a gun pointed to his head. But now, telling a girl you like her, you're feeling shy?"

Dave is grinning back now. "Stop it, Aquila, you'll make me blush."

"It's Duchess Aquila to you," she says.

"Duchess?"

"Are you busy, Dave? Maybe you could come back to my house and I could explain everything."

"Sure. Besides anything else, I'm wondering why you're looking so glamorous at this time in the morning. Shall I hail us a cab?"

"Actually, now that you're here, let's walk."

It's a sunny afternoon, and Dave and Aquila buy

iced coffees before strolling languidly in the direction of her house, their arms linked, the conversation flowing. They walk along the canal, delighting in the sights of blossoming cherry trees and willows along the banks, ducks swimming along with their ducklings, and fishermen waiting patiently at the water's edge. As they walk, Aquila tells Dave the truth about parting ways with Richard, and about her newfound wealth.

By the time they reach her house, she has told Dave everything, and he has listened attentively to the entirety of her story.

"So what you're telling me is that the woman I'm falling for isn't just beautiful... She's a wealthy heiress?" Dave says, as Aquila clicks the front door shut behind them.

"Falling for?" Aquila replies, turning to face him, her eyes lit up with desire.

At that, Dave gathers Aquila into his arms, tenderly stroking her hair, and kisses her, hard. "Since the moment I met you," he says, and kisses her again. A few moments later, he scoops her up into his arms and carries her upstairs.

As Aquila falls asleep that night, still wrapped in Dave's warm arms, she knows that she has fallen in love.

But when she wakes up only a few hours later, the morning sunlight only just beginning to peep through the curtains, Dave is no longer in the bed with her.

"Dave?" she calls out, her voice still croaky so soon after waking. "Are you making coffee?"

There's no answer.

"Dave?"

Aquila throws on her dressing gown and hurries down the stairs. *Perhaps he's in the garden,* she wonders, *or perhaps he popped to the shop to get breakfast.*

It takes a few hours – and a few unreturned phone calls – before Aquila fully accepts the reality of her situation. Dave is gone, and he isn't coming back.

CHAPTER FIFTEEN

That afternoon, Aquila sits in her beloved tutor Diane's library-like living room, working through the details of her parents' funeral planning. As blessed as she feels to have Diane's help, and as horrifying as the talk of coffins and cremations is, Aquila's mind seems to keep wandering back to Dave. To the smell of his neck; to the feeling of his hands running through her hair; to the taste of his lips. How could he just leave her, after a night like that. Aquila had been falling in love; the chemistry between them had been so palpable that it had seemed to fizz and crackle in every inch of her body. How could Dave not feel it too?

"Aquila? Hello?"

"Hmm?"

"I was asking you about the buffet. Whether you thought there'd be any dietary requirements to cater for?"

"Oh. Sorry. Um… no, I don't think so. Maybe some vegetarians?"

"You're half a world away, aren't you?"

"Sorry Diane. I hope you don't think I'm ungrateful. I'm just distracted. Honestly, I couldn't ask for a better teacher than you. I'm so thankful for your help."

"Aquila, darling," Diane replies. "You're like a daughter to me. You know I'll help you with anything you need. I care about you. And now… well, I'm more concerned for you than ever. You're completely alone, with no family to help you."

Aquila hesitates. Should she tell Diane about Dave? She likes to think that she can tell her anything, but, for some reason, she's too nervous to share this detail of her life just yet. Perhaps because she's embarrassed that she fell so easily and quickly. Perhaps because she's still hoping that he might come back.

"Thank you so much, Diane," she says, at last. "It means a lot to me. I know I can rely on you for anything. You're like a second mother to me. Thank you."

"You're very much welcome," Diane says with a smile,

before starting to gather up the paperwork spread out in front of them. "Alright, Aquila. I think that's enough for today. Why don't you go home and have a good rest: it'll be dark soon. I'll call you tomorrow to finalise some of these details, ok?"

"Alright then, Diane."

When Aquila returns home and finds the house empty, her phone still revealing no new messages or calls, her heart sinks. *I thought he'd come back,* she thinks, glumly, as she climbs into her bed alone. *Why didn't he come back?*

*

CHAPTER SIXTEEN

The following weekend, on the morning of the funeral, Charlotte arrives at Aquila's house early so that they can get ready together. Aquila opens the door to find her best friend wearing a simple shift dress in midnight black, her arms laden with coffees and pastries.

"Good morning, Duchess," she says, in a gentle voice. "Shall we start with breakfast?"

In the kitchen, Aquila picks absentmindedly at her croissant and explains the Dave situation to Charlotte. She knows she should eat, but her appetite has disappeared. Even the idea of the coffee makes her feel nauseous.

"I feel terrible," she says, fighting back the tears that are forming in the corners of her eyes. "This is the morning of my parents' funeral, and all I can think about is Dave! I'm a horrible person."

"You're not a horrible person," Charlotte says,

soothingly, while rubbing Aquila's hand. "You're a human being. You've been through so much lately, it's hardly surprising that losing something good has hit you hard."

Aquila manages a few bites of her croissant and a few sips of her coffee, then the girls head upstairs and get ready for the funeral. Aquila feels shaky, so Charlotte takes over and styles her hair into an elegant bun before helping to pick out an outfit.

"How about this?" she asks, holding up a long sleeved, jet-black wrap dress. It is 100% silk and far more expensive than any other dress that she owns. Aquila has only worn it once before: Cristina bought it for her for her sixth-form graduation ceremony. Her eyes begin to well with tears again as she pictures her mother and father watching her from the audience. Her father had clapped so loudly that, afterwards, his palms had been bright red.

"I don't know, the neckline is a little low for a funeral, don't you think?" Aquila says, stroking the smooth fabric between her fingers. "It is a beautiful dress though."

"You can wear a cami top underneath. And how

about this?" Charlotte picks up a necklace from Aquila's dressing table: a sparkling purple amethyst gem, on a delicate gold chain. Aquila had found it in Tina's room a few days earlier and taken it. Amethyst is her mother's birthstone, and this pendant was one of the first gifts her father ever bought for her. Before Aquila was born. Before money or alcohol or health was an issue.

"There, perfect," Charlotte says, gently sealing the clasp around Aquila's neck. The gem sparkles exquisitely against the jet black of the dress. "You look so beautiful, Duchess. Like a million dollars. But I guess a million dollars is nothing but small change to you now, eh?"

Aquila laughs. It's only a small chuckle, but it's the first laugh she's had in a while. "Are you really going to keep calling me Duchess?" she asks Charlotte, with an affectionate smile. "What does that make you? My Lady-in-waiting?"

Before Charlotte has time to reply, the doorbell rings.

"That'll be Diane," Aquila says.

"Ok, you stay here and get started on your make-up.

I'll go and let her in."

Aquila has just sat down and picked up her mascara wand when she hears the low rumble of a male voice and Charlotte's indignant reply.

"Well, well, well, you've got a lot of nerve showing up here again, today of all days!"

*

"Dave?" Aquila calls out, as she hurries down the staircase.

There he is, a bouquet of pink roses in his hand, gazing up at her with his beautiful, soulful eyes. Her heart flutters as his eyes travel the length of her body, taking her in, and she is so excited to see him that it takes her a moment to register that he's wearing hospital scrubs.

"Oh," she says, forlornly. "Richard. It's you."

"Aquila, can we talk in private?" he says, stepping past Charlotte and into the house.

The disappointment runs through Aquila's entire

body. She feels her shoulders stiffen, and folds her arms tightly. "Anything you want to say to me, you can say in front of my best friend," she says. Her voice emerges as cold as ice.

Richard glances at Charlotte awkwardly. Taking her best friend's lead, Charlotte's arms are folded in front of her chest too, and she fixes Richard with a stare piercing enough to kill.

"Well, I wanted to talk to you. I wanted to apologise."

"Today, of all days?" Charlotte says.

"What do you –" Richard begins, but his voice trails off as he takes in the sight of the two women, the heaviness of their expressions, each of them dressed entirely in black. "Aquila I'm… I'm so sorry. I just wanted to talk to you but I didn't… Can I come back again tomorrow? Take you out for breakfast, maybe?"

Aquila stares at the floor for a moment, not knowing the right thing to say. Eventually, Charlotte takes charge of the situation for her.

"Tomorrow's no good, she's got a meeting about a business proposal. She'll see you on Friday: take it or leave it."

Richard looks at Aquila for confirmation, but she says nothing. It's as though the words are stuck in her throat, and all she can do is stare dumbly at her feet. *Where's Dave?* she thinks. *Did Richard hear me call his name?*

"Friday is good," Richard says, eventually. "Friday morning. If that works for you too, Aquila?"

"It works for her," Charlotte replies, before Aquila can so much as nod. "But for now, if you don't mind, we're going to honour the lives of her parents."

With that, Charlotte opens the door and gestures towards it, fixing Richard with a cool gaze until, eventually, he walks through it, casting a final apologetic glance in Aquila's direction as he does so.

"See you on Friday, Aquila," he starts to say, but Charlotte slams the door behind him before he can get the words out.

"Wow, Charlotte," Aquila says. "Thank you… I was a little lost for words."

Charlotte grins at her friend. "No problem, Duchess. Didn't anybody ever tell you you've got to treat 'em mean to keep them keen? Anyway, let's get your things. Diane will be here any minute."

*

The following evening, Charlotte, Diane and Aquila are sitting at her kitchen table with a pile of papers, drawing up a business plan. With the funeral behind her and her inheritance from Donald secured, Aquila's mind has calmed enough for her to contemplate the future. The future that she has decided on involves setting up a car dealership business with Charlotte and Diane. After all, she thinks, she may as well put her newfound wealth to good use, and there are no two people she trusts and loves more in the world than Diane and Charlotte.

"I think this is almost ready, Diane," Charlotte says, eventually, gathering the papers into a pile. "What do you think?"

"I think this proposal is looking really promising," Diane says, smiling. "I'm so proud of you girls. One minute, you're a pair of giggling teenagers who think of nothing but boys. The next minute, you're business moguls ready to take on the world! Where does the time go?"

"We still find time to obsess about boys," Charlotte says with a smile. "Oh, and food, too!"

"Well, I think that's what we call a healthy, balanced life," Diane says, beaming at Charlotte with maternal warmth. It's important to sleep on important things like business plans. What do you say, girls? Shall we call it a day and order a takeaway?"

Aquila checks her watch and is surprised to see that it's almost eight p.m. She's forgotten to eat anything all day.

"I probably *should* eat," she says, "though I feel pretty queasy."

"You do?" Charlotte replies. "Not me. I'm starving. Let's get Chinese food!"

"Honestly, you know I love Chinese food, but just the thought of it is making me want to be sick."

"Poor Aquila," Diane says, rising from the table. "Do you have ginger tea in the cupboard? I'll make you some – it always settles my stomach when I feel sick."

"I think we do, somewhere," Aquila replies. "My mum used to drink ginger tea for the same reason." Aquila feels the sting of tears in her eyes as she recalls her mother, and how kindly she took care of her when she was ill. She swells with gratitude that she has Diane to look after her now.

"Don't worry, Duchess. You've had so much on your mind, it's normal to lose your appetite," Charlotte says. "But let me order all of our usual favourites, then while we're waiting, you can tell Diane and I all about Dave and Richard."

Aquila feels her cheeks redden, and she glances up at Diane, who is filling the kettle at the sink and searching the cupboards for teabags. She loves Diane and feels she could trust her with anything, but she has never discussed her love interests with her teacher before.

"Why don't you girls go on through into the living room while I make this tea?" Diane says, seeming to sense Aquila's hesitation. "I'll follow you through soon."

*

By the time the food has arrived, Aquila has relaxed enough to feel comfortable confiding in Diane. With a cosy blanket tucked around her and the hot cup of ginger tea cradled in her hands, the tightness in Aquila's chest and the nausea in her stomach fades enough that her mind seems to relax too, and her thoughts seem to tumble out of her mouth freely.

"I just don't understand why he left," she says, between sips of tea. "Everything was so perfect. How is it possible that things can feel so right and then someone can just... disappear?"

"That's just guys for you," Charlotte says, through a mouthful of chicken chow mein. "They see the world differently to us."

"That's true," Diane says, as she gently folds shredded Peking duck into a pancake, "but it's also important not to leap to any assumptions. After all, it has only been a few days since you've heard from him. It's a lot of time for you to spend worrying, but it's not a long time in the grand scheme of things. There might be a perfectly reasonable explanation."

"Oh, come on, Diane!" Charlotte says, offering the tub of chicken balls to Aquila. "What reasonable explanation could have been so important that he didn't have time to call her?"

Diane's brow furrows at this question. "That is the worrying part," she says. "It's hard to imagine a situation where he couldn't have called you."

Aquila picks at the chicken ball in her hand but she can't bring herself to eat it. "You're right," she says. "That's the bit I can't make sense of. Even if he changed his mind and didn't want anything to do with me... He just didn't seem like the kind of guy who would walk away without saying why."

"I told you," Charlotte says, popping a spring roll into her mouth, whole. "Men don't think like us."

"I suppose you're right."

The three women sit in silence for a while, listening to the crackling sound of the fire that Diane has lit for them, savouring the food and the presence of good friends.

"But," Charlotte says, "the big question is: what about Richard and this breakfast tomorrow?"

Aquila sighs. "I don't know. I mean, Richard and I had a huge fight and I told myself I'd never see him again. But that was because he was so rude about Dave, and it left me feeling that Richard was a horrible person. But maybe he was right, all along! Maybe he was just trying to protect me."

"So do you think you'll go?" Diane asks, a note of motherly concern in her voice. "All I'd advise is that you meet him in a public place. I don't entirely trust this man."

"Nor do I," Charlotte agrees. "But look. He's a handsome guy. He has a good job. And he clearly likes you. What have you got to lose, meeting him for breakfast?"

Aquila takes another sip of tea, placing the chicken ball back on her plate, untouched. "You're right. I suppose now I just have to think about what to wear. What do you wear on a breakfast date with a man you've already slept with, but that you aren't even sure you like?"

Charlotte grins. "That's exactly my area of speciality, Duchess. I'll help you pick out an outfit which is gonna knock him dead. Now –" she says, holding out a piece of sesame prawn toast and fixing Aquila with the same fierce look that she'd given Richard the day before. "Eat something. Before I lose my temper with you."

CHAPTER SEVENTEEN

By nine o'clock the following morning, Aquila is ready for her date and – although she still feels sick and has no appetite – she has to admit that she looks pretty fabulous. Charlotte has styled her in a black corduroy miniskirt which cinches in at her waist, and an elegant white blouse, unbuttoned just enough to reveal her mother's amethyst necklace glittering against her skin. Paired with black tights, knee-high boots, a swipe of cherry red lipstick and her hair styled into a chic bun, she feels like a Parisian model.

"Put your trench coat on," Charlotte had told her, before she left the house, "but leave it unbelted. You want to look formal and elegant, but with a hint of the sexy minx he knows you are, underneath."

Both Diane and Aquila had blushed at this comment, but even Diane had to admit that Charlotte was right.

"How did you learn all of this stuff?" Diane had said with an affectionate laugh. "And where were you when I was a teenage girl?"

Diane had given Charlotte a lift home, after reminding Aquila to keep them both updated on how things were going, and now Aquila was waiting on the staircase for Richard to arrive, her stomach fluttering with nervous excitement.

Richard was due to arrive at 9.15 a.m. At 9.14, his car pulls up on the front drive. Aquila steps outside to discover Richard waiting for her in a silver Mercedes-Benz soft top, the roof down.

"Is this the E-Class Cabriolet?" she asks him, entranced by the car's beauty, as she climbs into the passenger seat.

"A girl who knows her cars," Richard says, slinging his left arm casually over Aquila's shoulder, and using the other to reverse off of the driveway. "Very impressive."

"I know how much they cost, too," she says, an undeniable tingle of pleasure running through her body at the feeling of Richard's hand grazing her arm. *I need to suppress this feeling,* she thinks. *I can't let him know the effect he has on me.* "I suppose doctors must earn more than I thought."

"Either that or they make stupid financial decisions."

With this, Richard turns to smile at her. He's wearing Ray-Ban sunglasses which make it hard to tell what kind of mood he's in, but, even still, Aquila senses a significant change compared to two days ago. He's more confident; more assertive; more aloof.

"Where are we going for breakfast?" she asks.

"Did you like your roses?" he asks.

"Yes," she says, though the truth is that there were so many flowers delivered to the house on the day of the funeral that the roses had slipped her mind. "Thank you. It was good of you to come over and apologise. Are we having breakfast in town?"

"Well, I figured we both said some things we didn't mean," he says. "And a man should make the first move, when it comes to fixing things like this. A man should be the bigger person. We should let women be the emotional and sensitive ones."

"I suppose," Aquila says, though she doesn't like the edge to Richard's voice. "I probably shouldn't have been so quick to defend your brother. After all, I hardly know him."

Richard lets out a bitter laugh. "Trust me, there's a lot I could tell you about my brother. But I really don't want to waste time talking about that loser. Just trust me when I tell you that I'm only looking out for you. Dave is bad news, and the sooner you realise that, the better."

Aquila notices, with alarm, that Richard is merging onto the motorway.

"How far away is this breakfast place?" she asks Richard, looking with panic at the unfamiliar road signs around her. She may have picked up a few ideas about cars, but when it comes to the roads they drive on, Aquila is clueless.

"It's not far," Richard says, after a worryingly long pause. "We'll definitely be there for check-in at 12."

"Check in? Twelve? It's barely past nine, I –"

"Aquila, will you just trust me?" Richard says, squeezing her shoulder so firmly that she feels a bloom of pain in her arm. "You're going to love this place."

"What place?" She asks, unable to conceal the panic in her voice. "Where are you taking me?"

Richard sighs and releases Aquila's arm with a shrug of irritation. "It's supposed to be a surprise. Can't you let me surprise you?" he says.

"Richard, I have had enough surprises for one week. Tell me exactly what we're doing, right now." The words are brave, but her voice is as trembling and meek as a little girl asking if she can sleep in her parents' bed after watching a scary movie.

"Fine," he says, coldly. "If you want to ruin the surprise, that's fine." Richard takes a deep breath, shakes the irritation out of his voice and turns to Aquila with a warm smile. "I couldn't bear the idea of only seeing you for an hour or so in some boring cafe full of grannies and screaming kids. I wanted you all to myself, and I wanted to be able to take our time together. So I thought I'd surprise you with a minibreak. This way, we can spend the whole weekend together."

*

"We're here."

It's only when Richard shakes Aquila gently that she realises she has fallen asleep for the majority of the journey.

"Sorry, I... I didn't get much sleep last night," Aquila says. The truth is that she had tossed and turned in bed, wondering about Dave, worrying about her plans with Richard. Now, she realises, she was right to worry.

"Don't worry, sweetheart. I'm happy for you to be well rested. Now, what do you think?"

At Richard's words, Aquila looks up, and the sight of their destination takes her breath away. The driveway winds luxuriously along a long, tree-lined avenue, the sound of gravel crunching expensively under the wheels of the Mercedes, a beautiful Georgian manor emerging elegantly on the horizon. Eventually, they reach the building and Richard parks up alongside a grand stone fountain. While he takes a matching set of Louis Vuitton suitcases from the boot, Aquila marvels at the Greek statues and pillars which line the front of the house, as well as the roses and wisteria that adorn the vast double doors.

"M'lady," Richard says, opening the passenger door and offering a hand to Aquila. "May I show you to your room?"

From nowhere, a young man dressed in a sharp suit has arrived, holding out a tray with two glasses of champagne. Richard takes both and offers one to Aquila, while the young man silently bows and gathers the suitcases onto a metal trolley.

"To us," Richard says, raising his glass for a toast, his eyes glittering wickedly.

"To us," Aquila replies, tentatively, taking a sip of her drink.

As the young butler begins to walk in the direction of the double doors, Richard takes Aquila's hand in his.

"I know you're a woman with expensive tastes, Aquila. I want to show you that I can give you everything that you deserve."

I can give it to myself, a small voice in the back of Aquila's mind says, but it is drowned out by a second, louder voice. A voice that is taken in by the smell of Richard's aftershave, by the tart bubbles of the champagne, by the splendour of this opulent country manor.

"Now," Richard says, tugging lightly on Aquila's hand. "May I show you to your room?"

*

Some time later, Aquila and Richard lie together, wearing nothing except for the Egyptian cotton sheets which adorn the four-poster bed of their luxury suite. Richard's muscular arms are wrapped tightly and possessively around Aquila's narrow shoulders, her head nestled cosily into the nook beneath his chin, taking in the musky scent of his aftershave and the comforting rhythm of his beating heart.

"Making love to you makes me feel like a teenager again," Richard says, sighing deeply.

Making love? Aquila thinks, taken aback by the affectionate nature of Richard's words. Come to think of it, the way that Richard had held her just now – the tenderness of his kisses and the warmth in his eyes – did feel like making love. *But how?* She thinks. *How can this be the same cruel man I met in the hospital, who spoke so hatefully about his estranged brother?*

Aquila is distracted from her thoughts by a knock on the door.

"Come in!" Richard calls out, breezily.

"Richard! No!" Aquila protests, but it is too late. The bedroom door swings open and the young man who had carried their suitcases to their room is back again, pushing a heavily laden trolley into the room.

Blushing furiously, Aquila scrabbles to pull the blanket up over her naked body.

"Sorry, we were just…"

"Don't worry, Aquila, this man is a professional. He knows exactly what we were doing and I'm sure he's seen it all before!" Richard says, with a laugh.

Whatever the young man thinks remains a mystery. His face is completely expressionless and unmoved as he takes fine china plates and sparkling silverware from the trolley, arranging it precisely and silently on the dining table at the foot of the bed. Within a few minutes, all of which Aquila spends wishing that the ground would swallow her up, the young man has finished his task and, with a bow, silently leaves the room, clicking the door quietly shut behind him.

"Are you ready for some breakfast?" Richard asks.

Aquila pushes herself up onto her elbows to examine the spread. Arranged atop a white linen tablecloth is a bountiful array of breakfast foods: freshly squeezed orange juice in crystal tumblers; a sterling silver cafetiere of coffee; stacks of fluffy pancakes with an accompanying jug of syrup and a bowl of fresh berries; a rack of perfectly browned toast with neat pats of butter and pots of marmalade; a basket of freshly baked croissants and Danish pastries. It looks beautiful, and – for a moment – Aquila's eyes light up with excitement. But then, just as had been the case the night before with Charlotte and Diane, Aquila feels her stomach roil.

"Actually, I'm not," Aquila says. "Sorry, I just... I don't seem to have an appetite. I feel sick."

"Sick?"

"Yes."

"How long have you been feeling like this?" Richard asks, frowning with concern.

"On and off for the past week, to be honest," Aquila says. "I put it down to the emotional upheaval of everything that has been happening with my parents, you know. Plus the stress of organising the funeral, and I've been trying to throw my energy into a business proposal with my friends..."

"Have you considered that it might be morning sickness?"

"No, my period isn't due until..." Aquila trails off and her blood runs cold as she realises that her period was due two weeks ago.

How could I just forget? she thinks. She has been so wrapped up in the chaos of life that she had never pieced together the missing period, the constant nausea and, now that she thinks about it, the exhaustion she has felt for the last week.

Aquila is so stunned by this realisation that it takes her a good minute to say anything at all. How... How could she have not considered this most obvious of reasons for her relentless nausea?

"Aquila?"

Richard's voice, full of concern, snaps her out of her trance.

"Hmm? Sorry, I... I guess my mind was so full of other things that I... I didn't even..." Aquila's mind is whirling and whirring so much that she can hardly finish a sentence.

"Aquila." Richard's voice is firmer now, back to his normal, assertive self. "Aquila, don't worry. Let's not leap to any conclusions. I'm going to go to reception and see if they can find you a pregnancy test. Why don't you stay here and wait for me? Try the pancakes, hmm? Or some toast? Eating something should help with the nausea, even if you don't feel like it."

Before Aquila has a chance to respond, Richard has thrown on one of the expensive looking hotel dressing gowns and hurried out of the room, slamming the door behind him.

*

Fifteen minutes later, Aquila sits alone in the bathroom, reading the instructions for a pregnancy test. At her request, Richard is waiting in the bedroom outside. "But I want to find out with you!" he had said, but Aquila had talked him out of it. She needs some time alone to think. Some time to take in the enormity of what might be about to happen.

Is she ready to have a baby, on top of everything else that is happening in her life?

Even if all this stuff wasn't happening, is she ready?

If her mother was still here, she'd be pulling her hair out and saying, "But you're barely out of childhood yourself!"

And what if she decides she is ready? Does that mean she has to stay with Richard and raise a child with him, when she isn't even sure that she likes him?

And the biggest question of all: what if the baby isn't Richard's baby at all?

But there's no time to mull over any of these questions. There's no time to think at all, because there are already two blue lines forming on the display window of the testing stick. The instructions leave no room for doubt. One line = not pregnant. Two lines = pregnant.

She is going to have a baby.

Aquila stands up, wanting to hold the test stick up to the light to make sure she's read it right, but the room begins to spin.

"Oh God," she hears herself say, but it's as though the voice is coming from somebody else entirely. Stumbling, she grabs onto the sink cabinet to steady

AQUILA: THE ADVENTURES OF A YOUNG GIRL

herself, meeting her own gaze in the mirror. Her eyes look wild and frightened: the eyes of a terrified little girl. Not the eyes of a mother. *Oh, Aquila,* she says to her pathetic reflection. *What have you done?*

The sound of three firm knocks on the bathroom door pulls Aquila out of her trance.

"Just a minute!" Aquila says, her voice unsteady. She runs the cold tap and splashes some of the icy water onto her face. *You look a state, Aquila,* she tells herself. *Pull yourself together.* After pinching her cheeks to bring some colour to her complexion, then smoothing down her flyaway hairs with some more cold water, she takes a few deep breaths, practises a serene smile in the mirror and swings open the door to the bedroom.

"It was pos…" she begins, but her words are cut off by the sight before her.

Richard, still wearing his fluffy white dressing gown, is kneeling on the floor of the hotel room, his eyes wide and expectant, his arm outstretched towards Aquila, a sparkling diamond ring clasped between his finger and thumb.

"Aquila, will you marry me?"

CHAPTER EIGHTEEN

"But I just don't understand," Charlotte says, as she stirs two sachets of brown sugar into her coffee cup.

It is two days later and, home from her unexpected weekend away with Richard, Aquila has arranged a breakfast with Diane and Charlotte to fill them in on her double whammy of news.

"I know it's a lot to take in –" Aquila begins, but Charlotte interrupts.

"No, it's not a lot to take in. That's not the problem I'm having. The problem I'm having is that – two days ago – you couldn't stand this guy. In fact, you were mooning over his twin brother, claiming that Richard was some kind of monster."

"Charlotte," Diane warns, using the stern voice that she used to use when Charlotte and Aquila were gossiping rather than focusing on their Economics coursework, "watch your tone."

"My tone?" Charlotte retorts, dropping her teaspoon so that it clatters loudly against her saucer and a couple at a nearby table look over. "I don't think my tone is what's important here. I think what's important is that Aquila was supposed to be going out for breakfast with a man who she has BIG reservations about, but instead he essentially kidnapped her, under the guise of 'whisking her away on a minibreak', and now she's come home and told us she's having his baby and that they're getting married!"

The three women are silent for a while, and a waitress arrives to place three plates of pancakes in front of them.

"Can I get you anything else?" she says, the note of nervousness in her voice revealing the fact that she has picked up on the tension at the table.

"No, thank you. That's wonderful," Aquila says, unable to meet the waitress's eye. This was supposed to be a happy occasion – she was taking her two favourite people out for brunch in order to share her good news with them. She had envisioned them cooing excitedly over the sizeable rock sparkling on her ring finger, and perhaps shedding a few happy tears about her pregnancy, before joining her in fantasising about baby names, wedding venues and all of the other magical things that were soon to become her reality.

"I thought you'd be happy for me, after all that has happened to me lately," Aquila says, quietly.

"Well you were wrong," Charlotte says, folding her arms.

"Charlotte!" Diane says, tartly. "You're being unkind!"

"Unkind?" Charlotte scoffs. "Well, why don't you say something, if I'm being so unkind. Come on, you're the 'proper adult'", she adds, aggressively miming air quotes with her fingers. "What do you think about Aquila's news?"

Diane doesn't say anything for a moment. Instead, she takes a sip of her peppermint tea and furrows her brow, as though thinking deeply. The three plates of pancakes sit untouched between them as the silence on the table grows.

"Well," Diane says, eventually, "I can see why you're upset, Charlotte. It's certainly a lot to take in. This is very big news, Aquila."

"I know," Aquila says, touching her stomach pensively. "I know that."

"It's hard for me to say whether I'm happy for you or not, because it's so sudden."

"But I'm having a baby and I've got a fiancé!" Aquila protests, surprised that Diane seems to be taking Charlotte's side. "A fiancé who's a doctor, who takes me away on fancy minibreaks and has bought me a gorgeous diamond ring! How could any of that be bad?"

"Oh for God's sake, Aquila!" Charlotte spits, when Aquila mentions the ring. "How can you be so naive?"

"Charlotte!" Diane warns, raising her voice enough this time that a few of the surrounding tables have started to pay attention.

"How can you call ME naive?" Aquila replies, the rage building inside her like boiling water. "You're the same age as me! You've never even had a boyfriend, let alone a fiancé! You're probably just jealous that all of this is happening to me, while you're still alone, living with your parents!"

Charlotte opens her mouth to respond, but quickly seems to change her mind. Instead she stands up, the chair scraping loudly against the tiles of the cafe floor as she does so, and puts on her coat.

"I need to leave," she says, fixing Aquila with a look of pure hatred, "before I say something I really regret."

"What about your food?" Diane protests.

"Let her have it," Charlotte replies, gesturing towards Aquila, "seeing as she's eating for two anyway."

With that, Charlotte storms out of the cafe, the bell on the door tinkling sweetly as she bursts out onto the street and disappears from sight. Aquila sits in stunned silence for a few moments before promptly bursting into tears.

"Oh, Aquila," Diane says, gently. "It's ok. It's all going to be ok." She waves away the waitress who is returning to check on the table, and calmly rubs Aquila's back while she sobs.

"Diane, is she right?" she asks, once she has stopped crying enough to get a sentence out. "Am I being totally naive?"

"Well," Diane replies, with a voice which suggests she is choosing her words with care. "I'm not sure. I'd need to know a little more."

"Please, Diane," Aquila looks at her former teacher with the pleading eyes of a little girl. "Tell me what you think. I can take it."

"Hmm." Diane frowns a little, as though thinking carefully. "Ok. Well, first of all, I think that these are big decisions to make. Having a baby and getting married are not decisions that should be taken lightly. I'm not saying that you haven't thought about that, but there is a lot to consider. For one thing, you're very young. Are you sure you're ready to take on all this responsibility? For another thing, you've been through a lot of tragedy and trauma lately. Those kinds of things can lead people to make hasty decisions. Are you sure you're keeping this baby and marrying this man because it's what you want, and not because you're making choices to take away the sadness of what you've been through? After all, whatever you think of Richard, you haven't known him very long. Marrying somebody that you don't know very well is certainly a big risk, and having a baby adds extra pressure to that. Finally..." Diane's voice trails off, and she begins to nervously chew her thumbnail.

"Go on, Diane. I trust you. I want to hear your opinions," Aquila urges.

"Well, this is really your business, and it's not something you've spoken to me about directly, but I did gather a few things from your conversation with Charlotte the other night, at your house. As I understand it, you've been... *involved*... with both Richard and his twin brother Dave. Can you really be sure that Richard is this baby's father?"

CHAPTER NINETEEN

That evening is the first time Aquila has been alone for a while. For once, she's grateful for a bit of time to herself. Grateful for the opportunity to sit with her thoughts; to arrange and make sense of all the insanity that has rained down upon her over the past month. There is so much going on and so many ideas competing for her attention that she feels as though a crowd is chanting and yelling inside her brain, so loudly and relentlessly that she can't even begin to hear her own thoughts. *How am I even supposed to know what I want?* she thinks.

I want a bath, she decides, at last. It's not a big thought but at least it's something.

Aquila has always loved baths. The sensuality of it. The calm luxury. The tingling, expansive feeling of relaxation afterwards. Accordingly, she takes her time in selecting fragrant bath salts, lighting her favourite candles and choosing a relaxing playlist of ambient music – soothing pan pipes and tinkling piano notes. She turns out the lights so that the room is almost dark, except for the gentle flicker of the tealights. She almost forgets herself and goes to pour a large glass of red wine, but quickly remembers that she won't be drinking wine for a long time, and settles for a glass of sparkling water and fresh lime instead. Gingerly, she steps out of her clothes and examines her naked body in the mirror over the sink. It's too soon to detect any change to her body, she knows, but she touches her hand lightly to her stomach anyway.

"I have to get used to thinking about both of us, now, little one," she says to her reflection. "It can't all be just about me anymore."

As Aquila sinks into the warm, soapy bath, she inhales deeply in order to take in the scents of bergamot and geranium, then exhales a breath of deep relaxation. She has been in the water for less than 60 seconds before the doorbell rings. Three short, sharp rings – the familiar code of her best friend Charlotte.

Thank God, Aquila thinks, with a sigh of relief. She has always hated arguing with her best friend, and now that she has lost her mother and father, the idea of losing Charlotte is even more terrifying.

"I'm in the bath!" she calls out. "Let yourself in!"

Taking a deep breath, Aquila prepares for the confrontation which is about to hit. She hears Charlotte open the front door and listens to the sound of her removing her shoes in the entrance hall. Normally, Charlotte would be singing by now, or shouting something silly through the bathroom door. It's rare that Charlotte is quiet, but perhaps, Aquila thinks, their argument has made her bashful.

"I'm in the bath!" she calls out again. "You can come in!" Charlotte has seen Aquila naked plenty of times – there is no shame or privacy between the two of them. Not after all these years.

Aquila hears the creak of floorboards as Charlotte walks up the stairs; hears the soft sound of footsteps on the carpet of the landing outside the bathroom door, but Charlotte doesn't come in.

"Charlotte?" Aquila says, with a slight tremble in her voice. Only now is she beginning to doubt herself. Only now does she begin to think that it might have been a stupid idea to leave the front door unlocked, and to invite someone into the house while lying naked in the bath.

Charlotte – or whoever it is that has knocked on her

front door and silently entered her home – doesn't respond. Aquila is about to step out of the bath and grab her robe when the stranger on the landing raps lightly on the bathroom door.

"It's not Charlotte," says a male voice, difficult to identify through the closed door, "it's me."

*

The warm water of the bath does nothing to diminish the ice-cold chill that runs through Aquila's body at the sound of the male voice. She scans the room frantically, wondering what she can do to protect herself. She thinks about grabbing her phone and calling the police, but her phone is in the bedroom, connected to her music system. She thinks about whether anything within her reach could work as a weapon, but there's nothing – only a few glass bottles of bubble bath and a razor: not exactly foolproof weapons against a mysterious stranger.

"Aquila?" the voice says, and this time, it suddenly becomes clear who it is. "Can I… Can I come in?"

Richard! she thinks, her body flooding with relief. *Thank goodness!*

"Of course!" she calls out cheerfully, sinking back into the soapy water of the bath. "You scared me!"

The door opens, and in he comes. Perhaps it is the pregnancy hormones, but Aquila feels momentarily dazzled by the gorgeousness of her fiancé: the light stubble on his face; the sparkle in his eyes; his sheepish smile. *Charlotte was wrong,* Aquila thinks, *sometimes, you just know that somebody is the one.*

She is so overwhelmed by this rush of attraction that it takes a moment before Aquila realises that this is not her fiancé at all.

"It's you," she says, her voice suddenly filled with panic.

"Hi again, Aquila," Dave replies. "I'm back."

*

It takes approximately 60 seconds for Aquila's shock to dissipate enough for her anger to kick in.

"What on earth are you doing here?" she spits, furiously. "Why in God's name would you think it was ok to sneak into my house like this? Now turn around so that I can get dressed."

"I didn't sneak in! I rang the bell and you told me to come in!" Dave says, his eyes remaining firmly fixed on Aquila's.

"Do you really think that if I'd known it was you, I'd have invited you in? Now TURN AROUND!"

"Fine," he says, following Aquila's instruction and holding his hands up in surrender. "Not that I really see the point, at this stage."

"The point," Aquila replies, hastily pulling on her dressing gown, "is that you forfeited the right to see my naked body when you disappeared in the middle of the night and failed to contact me again."

"Aquila, I completely understand why you're upset with me. I do. But I came here tonight to explain. Will you at least let me do that? Maybe downstairs, with clothes on?"

Aquila hesitates. Part of her wants to kick Dave out of her house before he has the chance to utter another word. She knows that Richard would expect nothing less. But another part of her is curious. The part of her that believed Dave would never hurt her intentionally, that still believes that there must be some kind of innocent explanation.

"Ok," she says, at last. "Give me a few minutes to get myself together, then let's talk."

*

A few minutes later, Aquila wanders downstairs into the living room, where she finds Dave crouching in front of the hearth.

"You lit a fire," she says, observing the flames as they crackle and spit in the grate. Nobody has lit the fire since before her parents died. It was always her father's job.

"I did," he says. "One of the few benefits of army life: you become an expert in basic survival skills."

Aquila stays in the doorway, hesitant, while Dave takes a seat on the leather sofa, picking up a tumbler of whiskey from the side table.

"Where did you get that whiskey?" she asks, wondering if Dave has stumbled across some of her father's old stash.

"I brought it with me," he replies, coolly. "Would you like a glass?"

Aquila almost says yes but quickly stops herself. It's going to take some getting used to, denying herself all of the usual comforts that pregnancy won't allow.

"I'm fine," she says, still hovering in the doorway.

"Why don't you sit down?" Dave says, patting the seat at his side.

Aquila is tempted to join him there, but she knows she can't let him off that easily. Instead, she steps into the room and settles into her parents' old loveseat, tucking her feet underneath her and pulling a tartan blanket across her lap.

"Well?"

"Well," Dave says, and, for a moment, his usually calm and collected demeanour gives way to a nervous expression.

"I'm all ears," she says, widening her eyes

meaningfully, in a way she has seen Diane do in order to control a classroom of rowdy teenagers. Part of her, she has to admit, is enjoying the powerful sensation of making a 35-year-old man nervous.

"Well," he begins, inhaling and exhaling deeply, "I don't know if you remember me saying, on the night we met, that it was almost my seventh anniversary. I mean it would have been mine and Susie's anniversary... If she hadn't passed."

"I remember," Aquila says. She remembers vividly how Dave had looked as he recalled his wife. It was one of the first things that had drawn her to him: the tenderness and love in his eyes. He had seemed like a man capable of great love.

"Well, I think I told you that I always get a little bit... crazy, around our anniversary. See, Susie and I had a tradition of making a big deal of our anniversary: we'd go away somewhere special, drink cocktails, stay up late talking and playing cards, you know. So, around our anniversary, I always struggle."

"Ok..." Aquila says, though she really has no idea where this story is going.

"Anyway, a few of my army friends... on the first anniversary after Susie was gone, they decided to try and cheer me up. They took me away on a minibreak – a big group of us went to Dublin for a few nights, on mine and Susie's anniversary. I mean it wasn't exactly comparable with the kind of break that Susie and I used to go on, but it was good fun, you know? Me and the guys, playing pool, splashing out on fancy dinners, drinking ourselves stupid, putting the world to rights. That kind of thing. It was... It was really good of them. It really took my mind off how much I missed Susie."

"It sounds like you've got some good friends there," Aquila says, gently. Aquila is surprised with her response to the way Dave talks about his wife. *I should be jealous*, she thinks, *but I'm not. I'm touched. It's almost the opposite of hearing Richard talk so cruelly about his estranged brother.*

"I do," Dave says, sipping the last dregs of his whiskey and promptly pouring himself a second glassful. "Anyway, from then on, the guys decided that we should make it a tradition. Last year, when it would have been mine and Susie's sixth anniversary, they took me away to Havana!"

"Havana?" Aquila replies, astonished. "That must've been expensive!"

214

"I wouldn't know," Dave says. "The guys wouldn't let me put my hand in my wallet the whole time. Like I say, good friends. We spent the whole week drinking mojitos, listening to Cuban music and driving classic cars. It was incredible."

"Wow," Aquila says, and her mind drifts briefly to a fantasy of her and Dave, driving along the sunny coastline of Havana in a Chevrolet convertible, the wind blowing in her hair.

"Yeah. So this year, I knew that the guys were planning something. They were being sort of secretive about it, and I kept telling them that they really didn't have to bother. I told them that it was because I didn't want to keep relying on their generosity, but really…" Dave trails off, and Aquila becomes impatient to know what he is holding back from saying.

"What? What is it?"

"Really it was that I… I didn't want to go away from you."

Aquila blinks but says nothing. Still, this story is refusing to make sense for her.

"The thing is, the whole idea of the guys taking me on these trips is that they want to cheer me up about my anniversary with Susie. But the truth is, this year, I was already cheered up. Because of you."

Aquila can feel her cheeks reddening, and she hopes that it's too dark in the soft firelight for Dave to see her blush.

"I see," she says, not wanting to give away too much about how she's feeling. Not yet.

"Anyway, I didn't want to tell the guys about you, not yet. It was still early days, and things hadn't exactly been running smoothly between you and me. So I just told them that I didn't want to take advantage of their generosity, and that I'd be ok. But they… didn't believe me. They thought I was just being polite."

"I'm sorry, Dave, I still don't really understand where this is going."

"Well, that morning, after you and I had spent the night together… I was on cloud nine, Aquila. I really was. I woke up next to you… You looked so peaceful and beautiful lying there asleep next to me, and I just couldn't believe my luck. I went downstairs to make some coffee for us, but before I could, my phone rang. It was my friend Mike – I answered and he was practically screaming at me that he had an emergency and he needed me to come over straight away. Now, I think you can probably tell from what I've already told you… My buddies and I are always there for each other, no matter what. So I came back upstairs, threw my clothes on, grabbed my stuff and left."

"You just snuck out? You didn't think to tell me?"

"Aquila, it was barely six in the morning. I didn't want to disturb a sleeping angel. Besides, I had my phone and I thought I could call you as soon as I knew more about what was going on. It sounds stupid now, but Mike doesn't live far from you. I thought I could be back before you even woke up."

"Ok…" says Aquila, still not entirely free from suspicion. "So then what happened?"

"So it was a trick. All of it was one big lie. When I got to Mike's house, he tells me he needs to drive me somewhere and he'll explain on the way. He tells me to leave my phone at his house; he says we'll come back for it soon but he doesn't want anybody tracking us. Next thing I know, I'm at the airport. The guys were all there waiting with their suitcases. They'd even packed a bag for me and got hold of my passport."

"They'd stolen your passport from you?"

"Yeah, I mean, like I say, Aquila, these are army guys. They have their methods."

"So what, they just bundled you onto a plane and you didn't have a chance to tell me?"

"Pretty much! I mean, I tried to protest but it was all happening so fast, that I was on the plane before I'd even clocked that Mike had made me leave my phone at his house."

"So they kidnapped you!"

Dave laughs. "Well, I guess you could call it that."

"And where did you go?"

Dave looks sheepish, like a teenager whose mother has asked them to explain why they've been given detention. "Vegas," he says, at last.

Aquila takes a moment to process all this. These last

few days, while she has been wringing her heart out, trying to make sense of why Dave would disappear on her like that, assuming that he must have used her… while she was heartbroken enough to accept a marriage proposal from his brother: a man who – aside from his identical appearance – could not be more different to the kind, loving man who sits before her now, sipping whiskey on her sofa in front of a cosy fire… All this time, he was gambling in the Nevada desert with his friends, celebrating the memory of his dead wife.

"Oh my God," Aquila says, dumbly, not knowing what else to say. Because how can she tell him? How can she confess her engagement to Richard, when this has all been such a terrible misunderstanding?

"I know," he says. "They were just trying to be kind, you know? I didn't know how to tell them that I wanted to go home to you. I didn't know how to reach you. All I could think of was a stupid postcard, but clearly it never arrived."

Aquila's ears prick up at this. "Postcard?" she says.

"Yeah, I realised that I might not have your number but I did have your address. I sent you a postcard trying to explain, but I guess it never arrived."

Aquila says nothing, but hurries to the hall to the pile of junk mail that has been gathering by the front door. She's had so much of it lately – not to mention the sympathy cards, the legal documents and the endless bills – that she has barely flicked through it. She does so now, frantically, and there it is: a brightly coloured postcard from the Caesars Palace hotel in Las Vegas, with a Nevada postmark and a scrawled note from Dave, explaining exactly the story he has just recounted. The card was franked three days ago: the same morning that she found out she was pregnant – the same morning that she agreed to marry Richard.

"I'm so sorry," she says, stepping back into the cosy firelight of the living room.

"Sorry? Why are you sorry?" Dave asks. "It's me that should be sorry. You must have been so worried. You must have thought I'd just disappeared, but the truth is… I thought about you the whole time. I couldn't wait to get back and see you."

"I… missed you the whole time, too." Aquila says. Sheepishly, she returns to the loveseat, tucking herself back under the tartan blanket. "When did you get back?"

"A few hours ago. I went home so that I could shower, change, make myself presentable... Then I came straight to you."

"Oh," Aquila says, the guilty feeling in her stomach making her voice quiet and shy. "I'm... glad that you came."

"I'm glad too," Dave says, his voice as warm and smooth as honey. "Do you think you can forgive me, now that you've heard my story?"

Aquila nods, slowly.

Dave beams. "I'm so glad."

I should tell him, she thinks. *If I tell him now, he'll understand. He'll understand that it was all a silly misunderstanding, just like his Vegas trip.*

"Dave?"

"Yes?"

She wants to tell him. She can feel the words forming in her mouth, but she can't seem to bring herself to speak them out loud.

"Nothing," she says, at last.

"Ok," he says, with a laugh. "Now, I'm going to have another whiskey. Can I make you a drink?"

*

For a while, Aquila and Dave sit in silence. The log fire that Dave has lit in the grate fills the room with a cosy glow, the sound of crackling flames soothing Aquila's heart. She sips at the hot chocolate which he has made for her, and watches him swirl a tumbler of amber coloured whiskey.

"I missed you," he says, after a while.

Aquila hesitates before responding. "I missed you too," she says, at last.

"Being apart from you... It made me realise... It made me realise how much..." Dave's voice trails off, and the look in his eyes tells Aquila that he is too shy to finish the sentence he has begun.

"Say it," she commands, staring into his beautiful eyes, yearning for him to hold her. *How can it be,* she thinks, *that he is identical to Richard, but so much more*

AQUILA: THE ADVENTURES OF A YOUNG GIRL

gorgeous to me?

Dave laughs. "You make me shy," he says. "I ought to be old enough to not be intimidated by young girls like you."

Aquila laughs. She has never thought of herself as intimidating before. *Naïve,* Charlotte had said. *Young.* It's as though Dave sees something in her that other people don't. More power. More potential.

"Can I come and sit next to you?" he says.

Aquila nods, and Dave steps across the room to join her on the small loveseat in the corner of the living room. It's a cosy spot, all the more meaningful to Aquila seeing as – long, long ago – her parents were so fond of snuggling up together on it and completing crosswords together, in happier times. Aquila would sit on the rug at their feet, playing with her Barbie dolls and basking in the warm glow of the fireplace and her parents' love. Now it is Aquila who is snuggled up with someone: this man who smells so good that she wants to breathe him in; that she wants to taste his lips against hers.

Dave places his whiskey glass on the coffee table and loops his arm around Aquila, caressing her shoulder in a way that makes her whole body tingle.

"Say what you were going to say," Aquila murmurs, her voice much less confident this time. Dave makes her shy too, she realises.

"I was going to say that being apart from you made me realise," he murmurs, his eyes gazing into hers in such a way that she knows he is about to kiss her, "that I never want to be apart from you again."

As their lips meet, Aquila feels as though her whole body is melting. She knows at this moment that this is the man she desires; this is the man she wants to be with; this is the man that she wants to raise her child with.

Gently, Dave lifts Aquila and places her beneath him on the loveseat, untying her dressing gown and sighing at the sight of her naked body.

"I have been thinking about this and nothing else but this... every moment since I left you," he says, breathlessly.

Aquila knows that she should be asking Dave to stop. She should be telling him the truth about everything –

about Richard and the baby – but she can't bring herself to speak. All she can do is close her eyes and savour the sensation of his lips as he kisses her neck, and his thumb as he lightly traces circles around her nipples.

"Dave, I –" she begins, but stops herself as he leans back to pull his t-shirt over his head. She reaches her hands up to feel the matt of dark hair on his chest, and traces a finger slowly down his abdomen, along the faint trail of hair which leads from his belly button into his jeans.

A few moments later, he is inside her. Aquila and Dave take a deep breath in unison and, for a moment, the two of them lie completely still, savouring this moment of pleasure.

"I'm falling in love with you, Aquila."

"I'm falling in love with you too," Aquila replies, and there is no doubt in her mind that she is speaking the truth.

*

A little while later, Dave and Aquila are lying in contended silence, soaking up the warm glow of the fire and the pleasure of one another's company.

"Would you like another drink?" Aquila asks Dave, rising from the loveseat and gathering their cups.

"A coffee would be wonderful," Dave says, with a twinkling smile. "If I have any more of that whiskey, I'll fall asleep."

"You're more than welcome to stay over," Aquila says, smiling. She tries to make the offer sound light and casual, knowing that she'll be devastated if Dave decides to leave.

"I'd love to stay over," Dave replies, smiling even more, "but I'd rather not spend the whole time sleeping."

He winks devilishly, and Aquila has to restrain herself from giggling like a schoolgirl.

"Coffee it is then," she replies, and disappears into the kitchen.

First thing in the morning, I'll tell Richard, she thinks, as she boils the kettle and scoops spoonfuls of coffee into two mugs. Instantly, she remembers that caffeine is another thing that she needs to avoid, so she switches her mug for another camomile tea instead. *I'll tell him that it was a mistake. I got caught up in the moment, because of the pregnancy test. He won't like it, but I can't let that stop me. I'll ask Charlotte to help if he won't listen.* The kettle boils and Aquila carefully pours the hot water into the two mugs. *Once that's all out of the way,* she thinks, picking up the two mugs and walking back into the living room, *I'll tell Dave about the baby. Telling him that first would just complicate things.*

"No coffee for you?" Dave asks, as Aquila holds out the mug to him.

"Not for me," Aquila says, flashing a cheeky smile, "but don't worry. I'm a night owl. I'll stay up as long as you want to."

She giggles flirtatiously, but Dave doesn't laugh, not does he take the coffee cup from her outstretched hand. In fact, Dave's face has been drained of all colour and warmth. His voice, when he speaks, is equally cheerless.

"Aquila. Why are you wearing an engagement ring?"

*

It's all over so quickly that Aquila feels as though she has whiplash. Dave wastes no time shouting or screaming; he doesn't throw anything or threaten to hurt her. He simply puts his clothes back on and leaves, his cup of coffee untouched on the living room table.

"I thought I could trust you" is the only thing he says before stepping through the front door and out into the night.

"Dave, please, I can –" Aquila begins, but Dave is already slamming the door of his car and driving away.

Aquila returns to the living room, sits on the sofa and sobs. Eventually, when she has no tears left to cry, she picks up the phone and dials.

"Hello, it's me. Were you awake? I wanted to say that I'm sorry. You're right. I am naive. Will you come over?"

CHAPTER TWENTY

"You know, Aquila, you don't need either of these idiots," Charlotte says.

It is only half an hour later and her best friend is already here in the living room with her, wrapped in a blanket and sipping at the coffee left behind by Dave. It is as though their fight from earlier that day had never happened.

"I know," Aquila says, sighing. *I don't need them, but I want one of them,* she thinks to herself.

"I'm serious," Charlotte says. "You're rich enough that you don't need the help, and you've got Diane and me for support. You wouldn't be doing it alone, and you wouldn't be wasting your time on some deadbeat moron either."

"Harsh, Charlotte," Aquila says, though she's secretly fond of her best friend's sharp tongue, particularly now that it isn't being directed at her.

*

Over the days and weeks that follow, Aquila's mind drifts back to Dave approximately once an hour. She spends time with Charlotte and Diane; she works on developing the business; she spends time planning the wedding that she knows in her gut she doesn't want to go through with. All the while, wherever she is, whatever she's doing, her mind repeats *Dave, Dave, Dave.*

She can't talk about it with Charlotte. She knows what Charlotte will say: break it off with Richard and forget about Dave. Charlotte seems to have a magical power for forgetting about men that are no good for her, simply by deciding that it's the right thing to do. She can't talk about it with Diane, either. She loves Diane – Diane is like a mother to her. But there are certain things that you don't discuss with your mother, and this is one of them.

And – of course – she can't talk about it with Richard.

She and Richard have decided to move the wedding forward.

"What's the point in waiting?" Richard had said, when they visited a reception venue that had a cancellation only three weeks from then. "We know what we want,

AQUILA: THE ADVENTURES OF A YOUNG GIRL

and we can afford it. Besides, it's not like we have a huge number of guests to consider, and the sooner we do it, the smaller your belly will be."

Aquila had blushed at this comment; even the events planner who'd been showing them the venue had looked uncomfortable. But Richard had laughed uproariously, as though he'd just made an excellent joke, and they had paid a deposit there and then.

So it was confirmed. The wedding was three weeks away.

A day later, Aquila had tried to call Dave. *Perhaps it isn't too late,* she'd told herself. *Perhaps I could still convince him what a huge mistake this all is.* But the line had been dead. She tried again: it still didn't work. She tried once more: still nothing. It took her approximately five attempts – and five unsuccessful texts – before she realised that he'd blocked her.

Why? Aquila asked herself, as she made calls to florists and bridal boutiques, cake-makers and photographers, *Why do you still think it's worth listening to your heart? When have you ever been right so far?*

*

A week later, Charlotte and Aquila are sipping chai lattes in a cafe in town, laden with shopping. Nestled in among gift bags, tissue paper bundles and ribbon-bound boxes are thousands of pounds worth of wedding purchases. Aquila has treated Charlotte, as her Maid of Honour, to a dress of her choosing: Charlotte has plumped for an elegant, floor length gown in sage silk which compliments her golden hair and makes her look like a Grecian goddess. They've picked up a baby blue garter, teardrop pearl earrings and wedding-night lingerie in delicate white lace. Each of them has a pair of six inch heels for the big day. Just one of the pairs would, once upon a time, have taken them a year to save up for. Today, Aquila was able to pay for both in cash.

"Ahh," Charlotte says, taking a sip of her latte and leaning back in her chair. "I was ready for that. I never thought you'd hear me say this, but I'm all shopped out! But tell me, has Richard paid much towards any wedding stuff?"

"Not really," Aquila confesses, taking a bite of her cinnamon bun. "It sort of doesn't make sense, considering how much money I've got. And besides, it's not like it's *my* money."

Charlotte raises a sceptical eyebrow. "Do you really think that?" she asks, coolly, "or did Richard tell you that?"

Aquila feels her face flush, and picks up her chai latte to conceal it. "Well, Richard did say it. But I agree with him."

"I see," Charlotte says. "Well, I don't. It's your money, whether Richard approves of how you earned it or not."

"Well, I didn't exactly *earn* it."

"Aquila, it's YOUR MONEY!" Charlotte snaps. Seemingly regretting her outburst, she closes her eyes and takes a deep breath. "Sorry," she says. "I didn't mean to speak to you like that."

Aquila shifts in her chair uncomfortably. "It's ok," she says, though it's a white lie. Aquila is still getting used to the strange hormonal swings of pregnancy, and Charlotte's small outburst has made her feel as though she's going to cry.

Luckily, Charlotte seems to have picked up on this.

"Aquila, Duchess, my beautiful best friend," she says, stroking Aquila's knee affectionately. "I don't want to fall out with you again. I hated our argument, and I regretted all of the things I said in the heat of the moment. I just care about you. I want the best for you. I just hope... I hope that Richard does too."

"He does," Aquila says. "He wants what's best for me *and* our baby." She hopes that by speaking these words out loud, she might speak them into existence. But it doesn't feel that way at all. It feels like a lie.

"Have you... thought any more about Dave?" Charlotte asks, gently. "You seemed... You seemed really upset the other night, when I came over after he left."

"I was," Aquila says. This, at least, feels true. "But there's no use in even thinking about it, really. He's not interested in me anymore. He's blocked my number and everything."

"Blocked your number?" Charlotte says, incredulous. "Are you sure? Let me see."

Charlotte holds out her palm and, obediently, Aquila places her phone into it. Frowning, Charlotte taps at

Aquila's screen for a few minutes before eventually placing Aquila's phone back on the table between them.

"You're right," she says. "I can't believe it. He doesn't know what he's missing."

Aquila tries to force a brave smile. "I know," she says. "But now, can you see that it's better for me to just focus my energy on Richard and this wedding? After all, we are having a baby together. And besides, you might come to like him, soon. You're my best friend… Of course you're protective… But maybe he'll grow on you."

Aquila's not sure who she's trying to convince: her best friend or herself.

The two girls are quiet while they finish their drinks. Aquila finds herself enjoying the silence, and surprises herself by almost nodding off, there and then in the coffee shop.

"You're exhausted!" Charlotte notes, with the warm concern of a mother.

"I know, sorry," Aquila says. "It's common in the first trimester, apparently."

"So much for the Young Aquila!" Charlotte says, with a raised eyebrow. "Meet Granny Aquila, falling asleep at four p.m."

Aquila smiles.

"Listen, I'm going to call you a taxi, ok? You can head home and have a nap. Leave me to sort the bags. There's a few more things I want to get in town."

Aquila protests briefly, but Charlotte bats her away and calls the taxi. Within a few minutes, she's being bundled into a taxi, settling cosily into the backseat and fighting the urge to fall asleep there and then.

CHAPTER TWENTY ONE

Back in the coffee shop, Charlotte orders one more drink – a black Americano, this time – and returns to the cosy sofa. She glances around to make sure that Aquila definitely hasn't returned to collect a forgotten purse or to use the toilet one last time (that girl certainly needs to use the bathroom a lot these days!), then takes out her phone to begin her master plan.

Hi, she types, furtively, *you don't know me but you do know my best friend. My name is Charlotte and I'm reaching out because you've blocked Aquila's number and I'm not sure what else to do. Can you talk?*

Before she can change her mind, Charlotte hits send and puts her phone away. She leans back in her chair and takes a sip of her coffee, then almost spits it all back out at the sight of the man who's just walked through the door.

Richard.

What are the chances? she thinks, as she hunkers down

into her chair, hoping that he won't spot her. Luckily, after breezily ordering a flat white from the barista – complimenting her sleazily on her outfit in the process – he sinks down into an armchair a few metres away, facing in the opposite direction.

Far enough away that Charlotte is sure he won't spot her. Close enough for her to hear every word of his phone call.

"Jack?" he says, with the loud arrogance of a man who is completely unbothered by disturbing other people with his private business. "Can you talk, my man?"

Eurgh, Charlotte thinks, *what does Aquila see in this idiot?*

"Jack, I want to know if you're free in a fortnight's time. You are? Fantastic. Ok, tell me this: have you already got a nice suit, or do I need to fork out for one?"

Charlotte shudders at the sound of Richard's laugh. It's a cold laugh. A cruel laugh. A laugh which, Charlotte suspects, is at the expense of her best friend. Carefully, she leans over ever so slightly, to bring her ear closer to the edge of her chair, and to Richard's conversation.

"What do you mean, what am I talking about? Do you need me to spell it out? I'm getting married, buddy! Haha, I know, I know. Who is it? Who do you think it is!"

Charlotte has an overwhelming urge to get out of her chair, grab Richard by the collar and throttle him. Instead, she stays composed. *Don't get mad, get even.* She thinks to herself. Quietly, she reaches for her phone, finds the voice recording app and presses the record button. Gingerly, she slips the phone along the arm of her chair, the microphone pointing in the direction of Richard.

"See, you remember now," Richard is saying, as Charlotte refocuses her attention on his conversation. "Yes, I know I said that, but things have changed somewhat. HA! No, I don't mean I've fallen in love with her, you bloody idiot. I might be getting old but I'm not getting soft. No, things have changed *financially.*"

Richard slows down his voice and practically purrs this final word – *financially* – in a way that makes Charlotte's blood run cold.

"Yeah, I thought she was just a bit of fun, but now it turns out she's a bloody millionairess. Yeah! I know! Property, cash, the lot. Well, yes, that does make her more of a long-term prospect, doesn't it? Because if I marry a multi-millionairess, what does that make me?"

I can't believe I'm hearing this, Charlotte thinks. *I knew he was bad news, but I didn't think he was pure evil.*

"Look, Jack, I don't need the morality lecture from you, ok buddy? I've already got a mum, thanks. She's a pretty girl and she's young enough to marry again. Besides, even half of that money is enough to keep her in pretty dresses and handbags. And I can hang up my stethoscope and fly off into the sunset. Yeah, I'm thinking about Southeast Asia. The Thai islands are supposed to be nice, eh? And the women... Listen, brother, I've got to go. I'm actually supposed to be meeting someone here." Richard laughs again – that same vicious, hyena-like laugh. "Come on, I'm not married yet, am I? Plenty of time to sow my wild oats. But you'll be there, right, brother? Alright, cheers, my man."

Charlotte listens as Richard puts his phone away and exhales a deep breath of satisfaction. *I'm going to destroy you*, Charlotte thinks. *Aquila may have fallen for you, but*

I know exactly what you are. You'll have to take her from my cold, dead hands.

Charlotte stays in her armchair, nursing the same cup of black coffee until it turns cold. She watches as a pretty blonde girl in a tight fitted jumper, a plaid mini skirt and knee-high boots arrives and approaches Richard. From their stilted conversation, Charlotte ascertains that this is a first date, facilitated by a dating app. The girl seems nervous, and her voice suggests to Charlotte that she's even younger than Aquila. Nevertheless, within ten minutes, Richard has convinced her to sit on his lap. Within another five minutes, he has convinced her to go back to his apartment with him. Charlotte watches them leave, Richard's hand brazenly cupping the girl's bottom as they leave. Through the glass window of the shop front. she watches Richard pull the girl into a passionate kiss, his hands roving shamelessly over her breasts.

It's the middle of the afternoon! Charlotte thinks. *Has he got no shame?* Still, she manages to take out her phone and snap a couple of photos of the kiss. As she does so, her phone buzzes. It's a message from Dave.

Hi, Charlotte. Thanks for reaching out. I can talk. Where did you want to meet me?

*

Two days later, Charlotte visits Diane's home for the first time.

"It's different from how I expected," she says, looking round at the elegant arrangements of flowers in vases, the neatly framed modern art, the scented candles filling the room with the smell of peonies.

"What did you expect?" Diane asks, visibly amused. "A desk and a whiteboard?"

Diane makes tea and, once they've chatted for a while about this and that, Charlotte shows Diane the pictures and plays her the voice note.

"Oh my," Diane says, as they sit together at the kitchen table afterwards, clutching the mugs of tea. "I knew he was bad news, but this is really bad."

"I know," Charlotte says. "We need to tell her, don't we?"

Diane sighs. "If we tell her, it'll break the poor girl's heart."

"I know," Charlotte says, "but at least it'll break her heart quickly. If she stays with him, her heart will still break; it'll just be much slower."

Diane smiles affectionately at her former student. "You're a smart girl, Charlotte," she says. "Far smarter than you ever seemed in class."

Charlotte laughs. "I save it for special occasions," she says.

"I'm lucky to be going into business with you," Diane says.

Charlotte shrugs off the compliment. "Oh, I went to see Dave, too," Charlotte says. "I tried to explain things, but he was a bit noncommittal. I think he really likes Aquila, but I think he's been hurt before. I played him the voice note, too, but he didn't seem surprised. He also didn't seem to know anything about the baby."

"Oh, Charlotte!" Diane gasps. "You didn't tell him, did you?"

"Of course not," Charlotte says, rolling her eyes. "Didn't you just admit that I'm a smart girl? Besides, if he's going to pursue Aquila, I want it to be for her. Not out of some sense of duty."

"Hmm," Diane says, then sighs and takes a sip from her mug of tea.

"If we're going to tell her, we should tell her now," Charlotte says. "It'll be painful no matter when we do it, but the sooner we do it, the sooner she can forget about this wedding and start thinking about what's best for her and the baby."

Diane doesn't take much convincing. Before long, they're zipping up their coats and stepping out into the cool evening air.

"I can drive," Diane says, remotely unlocking her Mini. "We can come up with a plan on the way."

*

They've only been at Aquila's door a few seconds when it becomes clear that their plan was a mistake.

"Look," Aquila says, calmly and firmly, "I know you both mean well. I know you both want the best for me. But I've made my decision, ok?"

"But Aquila, if you'd just –" Diane tries.

"The last thing I want is another fall-out with you two. I *need* you both now, ok? I need you to be on my side."

"We're always on your side, Duchess," Charlotte says, pulling her phone out of her pocket. "That's why we need to tell you –"

"Whatever it is that you're going to tell me," Aquila interrupts, fixing her best friend with a pleading look, "is it going to hurt me? Because if it is, no matter what it is, I don't want to know."

Charlotte stares at Aquila, then glances briefly at Diane before returning her gaze to Aquila.

"But Aquila…" she begins, but her confidence that this is the right thing to do has faltered.

"Please, Charlotte, please Diane. I just want to be happy. I'm trying so hard to be happy. Won't you just help me be happy?"

Charlotte knows in her heart that Aquila isn't happy. It oozes out of every fibre of her being; it's in every note of her voice. Nevertheless, Aquila has to make her own choices in life, for better or for worse.

"Ok," she says, at last. "I'm here for you. I want you to be happy."

Aquila offers for the pair of them to come into the house for a drink and a sit down, but Diane waves away the offer.

"We should all get some rest," she says, decisively. "We need to be in the office tomorrow for 8.30 a.m. at the latest – we have a lot to go over."

"And I thought I'd escaped you as my teacher," Aquila says with a smile. "Goodnight, Diane. Goodnight, Charlotte."

As Aquila closes the front door, Charlotte listens to the sound of her best friend bolting the lock, shutting out the dangers of the night, just as she had shut out the dangerous truth that Charlotte had hoped to share with her.

Oh, Aquila, she thinks, as Diane's car pulls off the drive and winds off into the night, *what are we going to do with you?*

CHAPTER TWENTY TWO

On her wedding day morning, Aquila wakes to the sound of a soft knocking on her hotel room door.

"Who is it?" she calls out, stifling a yawn. After the incident with Dave and the bathtub, she's learned her lesson when it comes to inviting people into her bedroom at the sound of a knock.

But, for better or for worse, it isn't Dave.

"It's only me, bride to be!" Charlotte calls through the door, in a cheerful singsong.

"One minute!" Aquila replies, forcing herself out of her cosy king-size hotel bed in order to let her best friend in.

"Good morning, sunshine!" Charlotte says, brightly. "I brought the Duchess breakfast in bed! Why don't you get back under the covers so that I can spoil you?"

Aquila does as she's told and clambers back into bed,

pulling the blanket up to her chin to hold out the chilly morning air.

"It's a beautiful day out there," Charlotte says, as she places an array of pastries onto a serving plate and pours fresh orange juice into two glass tumblers. "It's a crisp one, but the sun is shining and the sky is blue!"

"Since when were you this cheerful in the morning?" Aquila asks, pushing herself up onto her elbows as Charlotte brings the plate of pastries over to the bed for her to choose from.

"What else would you expect from your Maid of Honour?" Charlotte asks, with mock concern. "Besides, I've had three coffees already this morning."

Aquila laughs. "I'm jealous. I miss coffee." She selects a chocolate croissant from the plate and takes a bite, spilling flakes of pastry onto the duvet.

"Well, I guess now you know why our teachers were always so obsessed with warning us against teen pregnancy," Charlotte says, brushing the pastry flakes off of the duvet with a tut and swiping a pain aux raisins for herself. "Talking of teachers, Diane will be here soon. Then we can start making ourselves beautiful!"

For a little while, the girls sit in silence, eating their pastries and sipping at their orange juice. Charlotte turns on the radio and searches with the dial until she finds a classical music station.

"You're a classical music fan now?" Aquila asks, raising an eyebrow.

"Sure," Charlotte says, breezily. "Isn't everyone? Besides, I'm trying to create a nice atmosphere for you on your wedding morning. You know, romantic, elegant vibes?"

It's only when Charlotte says this that Aquila realises that her friend's apparent positivity has a touch of mania to it.

"Charlotte... Are you ok?"

"Me? What do you mean?" Charlotte smiles a tight-lipped smile, and Aquila can't believe that it has taken her this long to notice how strained her best friend is.

Aquila doesn't answer. Part of her wants to ask her best friend what the matter is, but another part of her – buried deep down at the pit of her stomach – knows what the answer is, and isn't sure that she can bear to hear it.

"Nothing," Aquila says, at last, and she watches a wave of relief wash over Charlotte's face.

"Ok, good!" Charlotte says, placing her cup and plate down decisively. "Shall I get your outfit ready?"

As Charlotte busies herself rifling through bags and cases, pulling out jewellery boxes and make-up bags, Aquila sits quietly on the bed and starts to worry. She has felt sick ever since Charlotte woke her up, but she attributed this to morning sickness – a feeling that she has become accustomed to by now. But now, with space to sit with her thoughts in silence, she realises that this is something more.

It isn't nausea she's feeling. It's dread.

"Well here we go, Duchess!" Charlotte says, still using the same sing-song voice which now sounds utterly insincere to Aquila's more accustomed ears. "What do you think?"

Charlotte gestures to the outfit, arranged neatly on the wardrobe against the far wall. The dress is more opulent and elegant than anything Aquila has ever owned before: the fitted bodice is ivory lace with a deep neckline which plunges almost all the way to Aquila's waistline. The skirt consists of layer after layer of light tulle, which rustle and swish dramatically when Aquila wears it, making her feel like a Disney princess. Her veil is princess-like too, floor length, translucent and flecked with delicate pearls. Her shoes are ivory silk, the silver heels accented by angel wings. It is a 'no expense spared' outfit, and Aquila still can't quite believe she paid for it all in cash. Her own cash.

For a moment, the malevolent face of her benefactor, Donald, flashes before her eyes, and her stomach roils with disgust. Then she recalls herself running, breathlessly, along Donald's gravel drive and out into the night; the dreadful fear of isolation. And Dave, rescuing her. Her knight in shining armour, a simple man in a simple car, whose impact on her heart had been far from simple.

Aquila has all of the money she could wish for, a gorgeous fiancé, a beautiful wedding gown. But the one thing she truly desires has slipped from her grasp.

Why did you give up on me, Dave? she thinks.

"Good morning!"

Diane opens the door and greets Aquila with the

same bright, strained, sing-song voice that Charlotte used half an hour earlier. Ever the organised one, Diane is already dressed for the ceremony: a chic Chanel suit in candyfloss pink that would have cost her a month's salary if Aquila hadn't bought it for her.

"Well if it isn't the mother of the bride!" Charlotte says, beaming.

Charlotte and Diane have become much closer lately and, in amongst all of the confusion and misery that life has brought to Aquila over the past few weeks, it is one silver lining for which she is truly grateful.

"Well, 'mother of the bride' is a bit strong," Diane says, shyly. "I wouldn't want Aquila to think I was trying to –"

"Nonsense," Charlotte says firmly, with a wave of her freshly manicured hand. "For today at least, you are the Duchess's mother. And may I say, Mother, how fabulous you look in that Chanel suit?"

Diane blushes. "Well, I certainly feel it."

"I'm so glad you're walking me down the aisle," Aquila says to Diane. "I really wouldn't have it any other way."

Diane turns to look at Aquila then, and Aquila sees a look in her eye which conveys far more than words ever could. Guilt. Sadness. Desperation.

Aquila's heart sinks. She has to say something.

"Diane, what is it? What is it that you want to say?"

A look of panic flashes across Diane's face, and she exchanges a meaningful look with Charlotte. Eventually, it is Charlotte that speaks.

"Look, Aquila, we really weren't sure whether to say anything…" Charlotte begins.

"Maybe we still shouldn't," Diane warns, though her voice lacks its usual decisiveness.

"Diane, it's written all over our faces. No offence but you're about as good at hiding your feelings as a mood ring."

"Both of you," Aquila demands, firmly, "will you just spit it out and tell me what it is you're thinking?"

"Well…" Diane begins, sitting gingerly in an armchair by the window, "why don't you join us over here so that we can talk about it?"

With some trepidation, Aquila climbs out of bed and joins Diane, sitting in the armchair opposite her. Charlotte pulls a chair over from the dressing table and, for a moment, the three of them sit in tense silence. It's as though they're attending a job interview but no one is quite sure which one of them is the candidate.

"Well," Diane says at last, "we were both just wondering… if this was definitely… if this was definitely still what you wanted."

"What, this wedding?" Aquila replies, aghast. She can hardly believe that the two of them would dare to ask such a question, with the ceremony due to begin in only a few hours.

"Yes," Charlotte says. "I know it may not feel like it, but it isn't too late to back out of this. Not if it's… Not if you don't actually want to do it."

Aquila says nothing, too stunned to speak. What can she say that would put her best friends' minds at ease, but which would also be true?

"Charlotte's right," Diane says. "We don't want to upset you – far from it. We love you and we want you to be happy. And we want you to know that if this isn't what you want, it isn't too late to back out. We can get you out of here and deal with everything for you. The guests, the suppliers, everything."

Aquila feels hot tears rolling down her cheeks, and she is powerless to stop them.

"Why are you saying this now?" she asks, her voice as meek and quiet as a little girl. Sometimes, with the weight of everything, it's easy for her to forget that she is still 21 years old.

"Because," Diane says, "Charlotte told me last night about everything with Dave. If it's Dave that you want, and not Richard, then you shouldn't marry Richard. It isn't fair on him and it isn't fair on you."

"And what about the baby?" she asks, looking Diane squarely in the eye. "What's fair for the baby?"

"What the baby needs," Diane says, gently, "is love. And they will have that in spades, no matter what."

Charlotte takes both Diane and Aquila's hands in

hers at this point. "That's right," she says, softly. "The baby will have more love than they know what to do with, I promise you."

For a moment, Aquila considers it. She considers packing up the dress, checking out of the hotel and driving off into the horizon with her two best friends. Maybe she'd treat them all to flights somewhere – anywhere. The three of them could spend a week or two relaxing on a beach somewhere sunny and far away, and forget about this whole mess. Maybe Charlotte and Diane were right: maybe she and the baby had all the love they needed right here, in this room.

But the moment passes, and Aquila steels herself.

"No. I'm going to go ahead with it," she says, her voice cold and formal. "I'm going to marry Richard."

"But why?" Diane says, a note of desperation in her voice. "Why do you want to marry someone who doesn't make you happy?"

"Because," Aquila responds, hot tears springing in her eyes, "the person that I want doesn't want me. So what's the point in waiting around for him?"

"Aquila –" Charlotte begins.

"Enough!" Aquila fixes her best friend with a firm look and wipes the tears from her eyes before they can fall. "I know you're just trying to help, and I'm grateful. But this is the decision I've made: for me and the baby. Now please, can you just be on my side?"

"We're *always* on your side, Duchess," Charlotte says, rubbing her best friend's arm. "If this is what you've decided then I'm with you. And I'll still be with you if you change your mind."

"Thank you."

"Now," Charlotte says, snapping back into her efficient and pragmatic mode, "the hairdresser and the make-up artist will be here any minute. Let's get you in the shower, shall we?"

CHAPTER TWENTY THREE

The weather is cold and bright when the wedding car pulls up outside of the church. The old stone building looks beautiful against the bright backdrop of a pure blue sky, and sunlight sparkles and shimmers on the stained glass of the windows.

"What a picture perfect day," Diane says, taking Aquila's hand in hers and giving it a squeeze.

"Isn't it?" Aquila says. "I only wish…" She trails off. If she finishes the sentence, she might start crying and undo all the good work of the make-up artist.

"I know what you're thinking, Aquila, and you don't need to say it," Diane says, gently. "All I can say is that your mother and father would be so proud of you if they were here."

Aquila fights back tears as she imagines her mother and father, and what they would be doing if they were here. Her father would be fighting back tears and telling her how beautiful she was; how he couldn't believe that his precious baby girl was all grown up. Her mother would be fussing, no doubt, fretting about flowers and seating arrangements.

If only you could have held on just a little longer, Aquila thinks. *I could have helped you with all of your money worries, and you could have been at peace at last. You could have been a happy, loving couple again, like you were when I was little.*

"Aquila?" Charlotte's voice snaps Aquila out of her reverie. "Are you ready to go?"

With Charlotte's help, Aquila steps out of the wedding car and arranges her dress and veil. Charlotte tucks a flyaway curl behind Aquila's ear and dabs a smudge of eyeliner from the corner of her eye.

"No more tears, ok?" she says, firmly but lovingly. "This make-up wasn't cheap."

Aquila laughs. "Do you think we're ready?" she asks her best friend.

"I think so. Richard's best man has the rings. Uncle Paul has his reading ready. Aunty Betty's looking after the flower girls – I said I'd text her as soon as you were ready, and she'd bring them outside. The guests are seated. They're just waiting for you to arrive, and then the ceremony can begin."

Aquila takes a deep breath and looks from Charlotte to Diane and back again. "Ok. Shall we do this?"

"Let's do this," they both reply in unison.

Aunty Betty arrives a few moments later, and her face is so full of pride and love that Aquila feels as though she's her aunty too.

"Aquila. Don't you look fantastic? A million dollars! Can this really be the same shy young girl that I saw at my party only a month ago?"

"Don't make her blush, Aunty Betty, she wants to look beautiful as she walks down the aisle!" Charlotte scolds, lovingly.

"Oh, nonsense," Aunty Betty says. "A bride should know on her wedding day just how fabulous she looks. Isn't that right, girls?"

The two flower girls – Charlotte's nieces, wearing ballerina pink dresses and flower crowns – both nod enthusiastically.

"You look like a princess!" one of them says, blessing Aquila with a toothy grin.

"Well, she's more than a princess," Charlotte says, lovingly. "She's our Duchess."

*

A few moments later, the bridal party has gathered at the entrance to the church, and Charlotte has given the nod to the harpist, who is now plucking the first few tinkling notes of *Pachelbel's Canon*. Aquila can feel her heart pounding so hard that she worries that everybody will be able to see it through her chest. She closes her eyes and takes a few deep breaths. *Come on, Aquila,* she says to herself, *if you can survive the last month, you can do anything.*

When she opens her eyes again, Aquila feels as though she is hardly present. It is as though she is floating above this scene, looking down at herself dressed in a beautiful ivory gown. She sees Charlotte neatly spreading out the tulle and lace layers of her train on the stone cobbles, and sees her arrange the veil neatly to conceal her face, but it is as though it's happening to somebody else. She wants to ask for a glass of water and a chair to sit down on, but she knows it's too late.

"I love you!" Charlotte says.

"I love you too," she replies, though the voice seems to come from outside of her; it seems to come from somebody else.

"Are you ok?" Diane's voice – and the sharp squeeze of her hand – pulls Aquila back to reality. Suddenly she's back with her feet on the ground, watching Charlotte and the flower girls disappearing into the church.

"I'm… I'm ok. Just a little… nervous."

Diane's face is full of concern and love. "I think it's very normal to be nervous," she says, and Aquila remembers how reassuring Diane would be to her and the other students as they waited outside the exam hall. "But just remember," she adds, "you're not alone."

Diane loops her arm through Aquila's and steers her to face the church. For the first time since she visited the venue with Richard, Aquila sees inside: the great, sloped ceilings; the white roses and lilies lining the wooden pews; the enormous stained glass windows behind the altar. There, standing next to the vicar, bathed in technicolour light from the sun shining through the stained glass, is her husband to be. He's facing away from her, so all that Aquila can see of him is his sharply tailored black suit and the back of his head. To one side of him is his best man: a fellow doctor that Aquila has only met once, briefly, over coffee at Richard's house. To the right of him is the vicar, dressed in traditional white robes, his hands clasped, smiling benevolently in Aquila's direction. The sight of Richard, facing away from her, should be filling her with giddy delight, excited anticipation, butterflies. But all she feels is a deep, sickening dread.

Is this normal? she asks herself, but she daren't say the words to Diane.

Charlotte and the flower girls are almost at the altar now, and the harpist's twinkling melody is slowing down. The organist begins to play a few notes which resonate loudly through the church, and the harpist joins in, forming an elegant, romantic duet. It's the wedding march: Aquila's cue to begin walking towards the altar.

"Are you ready?" Diane asks.

Aquila cannot bring herself to speak, so she simply

nods. Diane steps forward, and – almost as though she is walking through a dream that she cannot wake up from – Aquila has begun walking down the aisle.

Focus on your breathing, Aquila, she tells herself, *focus on your breathing and the calm will follow. This is all a case of mind over matter. Look at the guests. Let them calm you.*

She looks out at the guests and realises how few people there are in attendance. Barely the first five rows have been filled, and even among that small number, Aquila recognises fewer than half of their faces.

I guess that's what you get for planning a shotgun wedding, she tells herself. She pushes down the thought that her mother and father – her only true blood family – aren't here.

They are here, Aquila tells herself. *Mum, Dad, I know you're here with me. I know you can see me. I know you're proud.*

Would they really be proud of you? Another voice, from deeper down inside of Aquila, asks quietly. *Would they really be proud of you if they knew that you were marrying a man that you despise, purely because you're pregnant and you're too much of a coward to do it alone?*

"Slow down, Aquila," Diane whispers, pulling Aquila out of her thoughts and back into the room. "Slow, gentle steps. Take the time to soak it all in."

Aquila listens to Diane's advice, casting her eyes around the room. It really is a beautiful church. Giant pillar candles frame the altar, and ivory ribbons, tied in elegant bows, festoon the pews. Aquila looks from guest to guest, trying her hardest to offer them a dazzling smile. The smile of a happy, blushing bride. She sees Charlotte's Uncle Paul, grinning proudly, and two of her friends from college, one in an emerald gown made of shimmering silk, the other in a shift dress of elegant navy lace. Their eyes widen as Aquila looks at them, and the girl in emerald mouths, 'You look amazing,' while brushing a tear from the corner of her eye.

You can do this, Aquila thinks, *you are surrounded by love.* The sight of her guests is helping to settle her, and she has almost convinced herself that this she is calm, she is happy, she is making the right choice – when the sight of one particular guest makes her blood run cold.

There, sitting at the end of one of the pews, dressed in a sharp suit of French grey, is Dave.

As her eyes meet his, Aquila feels as though her heart

might stop in her chest.

What is he doing here?

What does he want from me?

Does Richard know?

Still, she is staring into Dave's eyes, and she realises that she has stopped still. She is staring at Dave and he is mouthing something at her. *What is it? What is he trying to say?* At last, she makes it out.

"Don't do this."

"Aquila?" Diane whispers, sharply. "We need to keep going."

Aquila shakes from her trance and turns away from Dave, then continues stepping towards the altar. Once again, it is as though she is rising above the room. Can this really be happening to her, and not someone else? Richard is turning to look at her, to take in the sight of his bride to be. She watches, dazed, as he touches a hand to his heart, and his eyes travel the length of her body with what seems to be a mix of amazement and lust. She hears Diane whisper something reassuring as she releases Aquila's arm from hers and takes a seat in the front pew. She glances over to see Charlotte grinning at her supportively, one of the flower girls sitting on her lap, the other holding her hand.

"Good luck," Charlotte mouths.

"Ladies and gentlemen, we are gathered here today…" the vicar is saying, but Aquila can hardly take in the sound of these familiar words.

Her hands are sweating and clammy; her breathing is shallow; her heart is beating hard against her chest.

"You look incredible," Richard is telling her, quietly.

Am I smiling? Aquila wonders. It feels as though she has no control over her body, no way to know whether or not her distress is written all over her face. *Can he tell?* she wonders. *Surely, he must be able to hear my heart beating.* Her thoughts seem to be screaming so loudly that it feels as though he must be able to hear her out loud.

"Aquila?"

"Hmm?"

It is the voice of the vicar, not Richard, that finally pulls Aquila back down to earth, though both of them are staring at her with concern.

"Sorry, I... I was just a little... I'm nervous," she manages to say.

The vicar chuckles kindly. "Oh, don't worry, child. That's very normal. Perhaps a sip of water might help?"

Richard's best man, whose name has now completely slipped Aquila's mind, holds out a bottle of water. Aquila thanks him and gulps almost the whole bottle.

"It may be normal," Richard is saying quietly to the vicar, "but my fiancée is a particularly sensitive soul. As fragile as a porcelain doll, aren't you, darling?"

Aquila tries to reply, but no words come out. Instead, she simply opens and closes her mouth like a drowning fish.

"Now, shall we try again?" the vicar says, gesturing to Richard's best man to take the now empty water bottle from Aquila's hand.

"Now, Aquila, please repeat after me. I, Aquila

Lawrence..."

"I, Aquila Lawrence..."

The room is spinning. Aquila thinks. *I feel as though I'm on a merry-go-round.*

"... do take this man..."

"... do... take this man..."

Am I passing out? Aquila wonders, as her feet seem to buckle underneath her. Suddenly, her six-inch heels feel like six-foot stilts, swaying in a breeze. *Am I going to fall over in front of all these people?*

"... to be my lawfully wedded husband."

"I can't do this."

If not for the gasps that echo through the church, Aquila might hardly have known she had said those four little words. Four little words which were about to change everything, four little words which are about to save her.

"Sorry, my child, did you say that –"

"She didn't say anything," Richard interrupts, his voice full of quiet venom. "Did you, Aquila?"

"I…" Aquila's voice trails off, pathetically.

Luckily, Diane and Charlotte are both now standing up and stepping towards the altar.

"She said she can't do this," Charlotte is saying, her voice so clear and confident that it seems to ring off of the stone walls of the church. "So she isn't going to do it."

Yet more gasps erupt in response to Charlotte's outburst, and a cacophony of scandalised whispers bubbles up from the congregation.

"Nonsense!" Richard insists, scowling in Charlotte's direction. "She's just having a dizzy spell." At this, Richard takes Aquila's hands in his and squeezes them.

To anybody watching from the pews, this hand squeeze might look affectionate, loving, reassuring. In reality though, Richard is gripping so tightly that Aquila feels as though her bones might break. This is not affection: this is a warning. *He's trying to frighten me. He's trying to bully me into carrying on,* she thinks.

Unfortunately for Richard, the violent squeeze has the opposite effect: Aquila feels as though she has had a glass of ice-cold water thrown into her face. By trying to intimidate her, Richard has woken her up.

"I can't do this," she repeats, but this time her voice is loud enough that there is no mistaking it. "I won't do this," she adds, decisively. "Not with him."

"Not with *me?*" Richard says, his voice full of disgust. "Do you hear yourself, Aquila? I'm a respected doctor, willing to lower myself enough to marry some idiotic whore that was stupid enough to let herself get knocked up by –"

"That's enough!" Diane shouts, with the firm voice of a woman who has disciplined legions of unruly teenagers.

"I think we all need to calm down and take a moment to remember where we are," the vicar is saying, but there is no hope of controlling the room now.

People are standing up and walking towards the altar, others are leaving the church, and the remainder have exploded into a chorus of shocked voices. Aquila hears the sound of a child crying, and realises that one of the flower girls is sobbing into Aunty Betty's bosom.

Where is he? Aquila thinks, looking wildly round at the chaos of the scene that she has created, but she can't see him. He's not in his pew anymore. Did he leave? Before she can think for too long though, Richard is yanking her arm, pulling her attention back to him.

"You evil little slut," he says, fixing her with a look of pure hatred. "You'll pay for –"

SMACK!

Richard's words are interrupted by a punch to the side of the head – a punch so forceful and sudden that Richard collapses to the ground in a heap, moaning and clutching his cheek.

"Speak to Aquila like that again, and I'll hit you even harder," Dave growls.

Aquila is speechless. She glances round the room to survey the scene, hardly able to believe her eyes. The guests that had stood up from their seats are slowly sitting back down again, eyes wide, as though settling in for a show. *They might as well have tubs of popcorn,* Aquila thinks. All the noise and chaos that dominated the room before is gone now, too. In fact, the church is almost silent, except for the sound of Richard gently moaning on the floor. For a moment, it feels as though time has stood still. Everyone is staring in her direction, silent, as though caught in a freeze frame. *What must they be thinking?* Aquila wonders to herself. *Most of these people don't even know that Richard has an identical twin.*

At last, it's Richard that breaks the silence, pushing himself to his feet and brushing the dust from his expensive suit.

"Well, brother," he says, looking at Dave with undisguised loathing, "you're welcome to her." He gives Aquila one final look and shakes his head with disgust. "I must've been out of my mind."

With that, Richard turns on his heel, hurries down the aisle and is gone from the church before Aquila can even respond. Richard's best man, whose name she has just remembered as Charlie, throws an apologetic, confused glance in Aquila's direction before running down the aisle in pursuit of his jilted friend.

Everybody else stays in their seats, totally still. It's as though they're waiting for something to happen; waiting for somebody to take charge of the scene.

Aquila turns to the vicar, but the poor man looks too stunned to move, let alone speak. *Diane is used to dealing with unruly crowds,* Aquila thinks, *but this poor chap has probably never seen anything like this in his life.*

It's Dave who – eventually – breaks the silence.

"Aquila," he says, taking both of her hands in his, her palm slotting into his like a hand in a glove. "My beautiful, perfect Aquila."

This is how it's supposed to feel, Aquila thinks to herself. The room seems to sharpen around her; all of the colours seem to brighten and sparkle and her whole body seems to tingle and fizz. *I may be young and naive, but I know one thing, at least. This is what love is.*

"Dave," she says, and his name sounds like magic.

"Aquila, ever since I first laid eyes on you, I knew that you were going to turn my world upside down. I knew that no matter where you led me, I would have to follow. I've had a difficult few years, but meeting you has made me feel alive again."

Aquila can't take her eyes away from Dave, but she can feel the anticipation and tension fizzing and bubbling in the room.

"I feel the same," Aquila says, and as the words leave her mouth, she knows that she has never been surer of anything in her life.

"Sir," Dave says, turning to the vicar, who looks as though he has just seen a ghost, "I am so sorry for the chaos that has unfolded here today, in this holy place. But I ask that you'll permit me one more act of madness."

With that, and to the collective gasp of the congregation, Dave drops down on one knee.

"I don't have a ring to give you, Aquila," Dave says, still holding on to her hands, "not now, at least. But I do have my whole heart. Everything I have is yours. I know now what it feels like to be without you; I know that I never want to go back to that place again, and I never want to let you out of my sight again."

Dave pauses here to take a deep breath. The room is so quiet that Aquila can hear the sound of silk dresses and tailored suits shuffling against the wood of the pews, as people lean forward in anticipation of the words that Dave is about to utter.

"Aquila Lawrence," Dave says, at last, "will you marry me?"

Aquila's heart is so full that she feels as though it might burst out of her chest.

"Yes," she says. "I'll marry you!"

At this, the room bursts into life again. There are cheers and rounds of applause ringing from the pews, the sound of Charlotte and Diane's voices chattering happily, the sound of the flower girls squealing and shrieking with delight. But to Aquila, there is only Dave. Dave's arms wrapping around her, enclosing her in a warm embrace that feels like home. Dave's lips pressing against hers, their kiss so full of passion and desire that she almost forgets that they have an audience, and that they're in a church. Dave's eyes, as he pulls back from their kiss to look at her with such tenderness, such kindness and adoration, that she knows – with every inch of her body – that she has made the right choice. That her life is just beginning, and she can't wait to see what the future will bring.

CHAPTER TWENTY FOUR

Ten Years Later

I t is a rainy Sunday afternoon, and Aquila is just putting the finishing touches to Sunday lunch. Cooking for her family is one of Aquila's greatest pleasures in life, particularly now that the business is doing so well and she's spending so much time at the office with Charlotte and Diane. They've already opened three branches, and they hope to open their fourth before the new baby arrives.

"Girls! Come and help me to lay the table please!"

Tina – nine years old and full of energy, just like Aquila when she was a little girl – comes bursting into the kitchen.

"Here, Mama!" she says, with a voice so sweet that Aquila's heart melts. If she thought she knew love before, it was nothing in comparison to her adoration for her sweet daughters.

"Where's your sister?" Aquila asks, ruffling Tina's

hair affectionately.

"Susie's coming in a minute," Tina replies. "Daddy's just helping her with the last part of her maths homework. I told her I'd do her chores for her."

Aquila smiles. Of the two of them, Aquila has always been the better mathematician – perhaps it's due to her work on the business – but Dave makes it a point of pride to help his little girls with their homework.

"You're such a good girl," Aquila says to her daughter, handing her place mats and cutlery to arrange on the dinner table. Her eldest daughter has always taken great pride in being the responsible one: she even packs her daddy's lunch for him now, and loves to braid Susie's hair in plaits on school days.

"Well, I just want to make sure that she's finished her homework so that we can all play board games after dinner," Tina says. "Ooh!" she squeals, excitedly. "You've given me spoons! Does this mean there's dessert?"

Aquila laughs. Tina has a sweet tooth, just like her grandmother did. She has her grandmother's eyes, too. *How I wish my parents could meet my little girls,* Aquila thinks, though she's reassured by the belief that her parents are looking down on her, proudly, from heaven.

"There *is* dessert!" Aquila says. "Peach crumble and custard: your favourite."

Tina jumps up and down on the spot with joy, and Aquila laughs. *Is there anything more wonderful in the whole world than the unbridled happiness of a child?*

Aquila bends over by the oven and pulls out the trays of food within: crispy, garlicky potatoes, carrots roasted in honey and thyme, and a leg of lamb, studded with cloves and sprigs of rosemary.

"Wait, Mama," Tina warns, sternly. "Should you be bending down like that in your condition?"

Aquila laughs. "In my condition?" she says, placing the trays down on the countertop. "Who taught you that phrase?"

Tina blushes. She doesn't like it when people remind her that she's only a little girl, and that certain phrases sound strange coming out of her innocent mouth. "Daddy said it," she says, shyly. "He says that women in your condition should be putting their feet up and getting lots of rest."

Aquila laughs again. "Maybe Daddy's right," she says, touching her hand to her bump, protectively. "I've never been very good at slowing down. But hey – old habits die hard, and you and Susie turned out alright, didn't you?"

*

Ten minutes later, the family of four – soon to be a family of five – are gathered at the dining table. Dave is carving the meat while Tina, kneeling on her chair so that she can reach more easily, is carefully doling out spoonfuls of carrots and potatoes onto each of their plates.

"Can I have some peach crumble first?" Susie asks, revealing a gap-toothed smile so adorable that it would warm even the coldest of hearts.

"A girl after my own heart," Dave says, smiling. "I sometimes wish I could live on peach crumble. But let's have some vegetables first, eh?" Dave winks at his little girl and Aquila's heart melts. Watching her family talk is one of the most soothing sights in the whole world.

It's rare that Aquila takes a step back from her busy life to appreciate all that she has, but when she does, she can hardly believe her luck. Her gorgeous husband is in his mid-40s now and, though the salt and pepper flecks in his hair are starting to reveal his age, the love and passion between them means that strangers in the street regularly mistake them for newlyweds. Her daughters are beautiful, kind and smart little girls. Tina loves books and baking and dinosaurs, and Susie loves building pillow forts, gymnastics and learning about space. They adore one another, and rarely argue – except for when they're trying to decide what to call their little brother.

Aquila never imagined she'd have a beautiful family like this, nor did she imagine she'd be an entrepreneur, managing a thriving business with her two best friends. She would trust Diane and Charlotte with her life, and she still can't quite believe that she gets to spend all of her working days with her two favourite women. Every morning, when she arrives at the office, she thanks her lucky stars for her second family: her home away from home.

"Do you want gravy, mummy?" Susie asks, carefully lifting the jug and looking at her mother with her enormous, puppy-dog eyes. Of their two daughters,

Susie looks more like her: they have the same eyes and the same hair, but her beautiful smile is all her father's.

"Yes please, sweetheart."

As her family tuck into their food, Aquila breathes in a deep sigh of contentment: contentment with her life, contentment with her work, contentment with her home. Sometimes she forgets that this home was once the property of Donald – she and Dave have remodelled and redecorated it so extensively to their own tastes that it is now flooded with light and life, as opposed to the dark, shadowy lair that it once had been. She still visits Donald's grave from time to time, to thank him for what he gave her. Dave doesn't exactly approve, but he has never been one to stand in the way of Aquila's wishes. Dave is protective of his wife and thinks there is no need to thank such a violent and cruel man.

Nevertheless, if Aquila could take that violent, terrifying night back, she wouldn't. If it hadn't been for that night, she would never have learned what she was capable of surviving. She would never have met Dave, and would never have had these daughters. She wouldn't have her business, and she wouldn't have her home. No, if Aquila could turn back time, she wouldn't change a thing.

"Right, everybody," Dave says, "let's tuck in!"

"Wait, please," Aquila says, raising her glass of sparkling water. "Let's have a toast first."

The girls raise their own glasses of juice, carefully imitating their mother's pose, and Dave raises his glass of red wine.

"To family, to love, and to being grateful for what we have," Aquila says, beaming at her beloved family and touching a hand to her bump.

"To family, to love, and to being grateful for what we have!" her family reply, in unison, and the room fills with the sound of clinking glasses and laughter.

Then, just as Aquila is about to pick up her cutlery and begin her meal, she feels something against her palm. For the first time, as though he has decided to join in with their toast, Aquila feels the baby kick.

StoryTerrace

Printed in Great Britain
by Amazon